IDENTITY THEFT TOOLKIT
How to Recover From and Avoid Identity Theft

John Lenardon

A 2008 Gift from

Stockton Cheese, Inc.

Self-Couns
(a division of
Internation
USA   Cana...

Self-Counsel Press acknowledges the financial support of the Government of Canada through the Book Publishing Industry Development Program (BPIDP) for our publishing activities.

Printed in Canada.

First edition: 2006

Library and Archives Canada Cataloguing in Publication

Lenardon, John, 1952–
  Identity theft toolkit : how to recover from and avoid identity theft / John Lenardon.

(Self-counsel reference series)
Accompanied by a CD-ROM.
ISBN-13: 978-1-55180-689-1
ISBN-10: 1-55180-689-4

  1. Identity theft. 2. Identity theft--Prevention. I. Title.
II. Series.

HV6675.L45 2006   364.16'3   C2006-900196-0

Special thanks to my editor, Catherine Plear, whose ideas and attention to detail contributed greatly to the book.

Self-Counsel Press
(a division of)
International Self-Counsel Press Ltd.

1704 North State Street   1481 Charlotte Road
Bellingham, WA 98225   North Vancouver, BC V7J 1H1
          USA   Canada

To my dog, Beau, who thinks I am perfect.

And above all to my wife, Caroline,
who loves me enough to remind me I'm not there yet.
Without them, life would never be as good.

CONTENTS

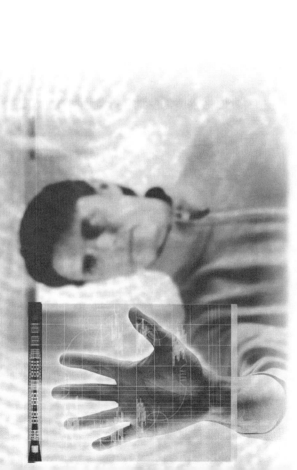

NOTICE TO READERS

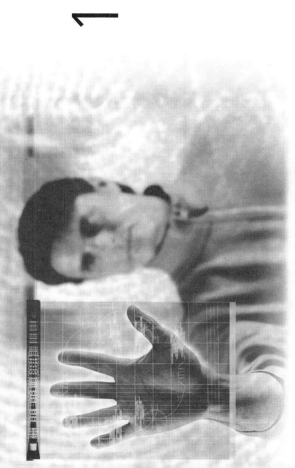

WHAT IS IDENTITY THEFT?

Identity theft is the fastest-growing nonviolent crime in North America today. When someone steals personal information from you such as your driver's license number, social security number, or social insurance number, or other identifying information to use for illegal purposes, you have become a victim of identity theft.

The thief could use your personal information to apply for credit cards in your name or open a checking account and write bad checks in your name. Your credit rating and your reputation could be severely damaged.

Victims of identity theft often suffer substantial economic and emotional harm. A victim will spend significant amounts of time fighting problems such as bounced checks, loan denials, credit card application rejections, and debt-collection harassment. Many victims also report feeling personally violated.

Thieves have stolen identities of teens and changed the birth dates. In some cases, teenagers applying for college loans have been told their credit rating was destroyed years ago.

There have even been cases in which an identity thief used the victim's name when caught during a criminal act. Some ID theft victims face criminal investigation, arrest, or conviction because of the thieves' activities. For example, one victim was the subject of an arrest warrant based on speeding tickets issued to an ID thief. Some victims have also been denied employment or lost their jobs as a result of their identities having been stolen and used in illegal activities.

On April 13, 2005, Chris Swecker, the assistant director of the Criminal Investigative Division, Federal Bureau of Investigation, appeared before the Senate Judiciary Committee.

He stated, "Identity theft has emerged as one of the dominant white-collar crime problems of the 21st century. Estimates vary regarding the true impact of the problem, but agreement exists that it is pervasive and growing. In addition to the significant harm caused to the monetary victims of the frauds, often providers of financial, governmental or other services, or the individual victim of the identity theft may experience a severe loss in their ability to utilize their credit and their financial identity."

A report to the Attorney General of the United States and the Minister of Public Safety and Emergency Preparedness Canada indicated that identity theft was growing rapidly, due in part to the Internet and modern technology.

During a one-year period, total losses to individuals and businesses related to identity theft in the United States were estimated at approximately US $53 billion. In Canada, the losses for the same period were estimated at approximately CDN $2.5 billion.

A US Federal Trade Commission identity theft survey found that victims had spent a total of 300 million hours in the preceding year to resolve problems created by the theft of their identities.

All the current data show that identity theft will continue to grow substantially over the next decade and pose a threat to tens of millions of people and businesses in Canada and the United States.

WHAT DOES PERSONAL INFORMATION INCLUDE?

Any information that describes or identifies you is considered personal information.

This information could exist in any number of forms. For example, you may have had an ID-badge picture taken at work, paid a parking ticket, applied for credit cards or a mortgage, or bought a car. In each case, you have released some personal information.

Some of this information is harmless and is useless to identity thieves. However, some of it is dangerous and needs to be controlled and protected.

Some examples of personal information that you should protect are your —

- birth date,
- city of birth,
- driver's license number,
- passport number,
- home address,
- social security number or social insurance number,
- phone numbers,
- e-mail addresses, and
- family members' names and birth dates.

More than ever before, companies and governments are asking for your personal data. Every time you apply for credit, get a new job, make travel arrangements, or even make a purchase at a store, someone is demanding your information. Unfortunately, every time you release this information, the risk that it will be stolen increases. You could spend months or years trying to clear your name.

No computer system is guaranteed secure. Some of the largest companies in the world have had client records stolen. So have government agencies and employers. No organization can fully protect your data from the constant attacks they face.

Identity theft has become big business for criminals. The amount of money involved is enormous and increases each year. As the criminal profits grow, so will the attacks.

It's up to you to learn how to protect your personal information and do everything you can to ensure it never is used to steal your identity.

IDENTITY THEFT AND TECHNOLOGY

Today, our personal data is more vulnerable than ever. It isn't something you can replace. It can't be insured nor can it be locked up in a safe. Once it is stolen, it is "out there" forever, and you can never be certain it will be safe again.

We live in an age of technology in which everything seems possible. We can store millions of records on a device that can fit in your pocket, and a single laptop computer can store hundreds of thousands of client records. In addition, almost every computer in the world is connected to public communication lines.

Unfortunately, there is one very weak link in all this technology. We can't completely protect the data. The tighter we make security, the less efficient the systems become. We could go to the extreme and lock up the data so that no one can access it, but such a step is neither economical nor sensible. Therefore, we must always compromise. In most cases, the need for easy access to the data outweighs the danger of it being stolen.

Some organizations demand access to our personal information, and others ask for it, but the result for us is the same. Whenever we give them any of our personal information, it becomes easier to steal.

Personal information has been stolen from all kinds of organizations including government departments and credit reporting agencies. The very people who publish long, detailed policies on how they will protect our data are incapable of doing so, and it is unlikely this situation will change.

HOW DO IDENTITY THIEVES STEAL INFORMATION?

Although technology can make it difficult for you to protect your information, it is only part of the problem. Identity thieves often use surprisingly low-tech methods to obtain your personal information. For instance, they steal your wallet or purse, or they steal mail from your mailbox.

Or a thief will break into your car or house. In many of these cases, the real reason behind the break-in is not to steal your personal property; it is to steal your personal information.

What follows here is a list of some of the most common methods used by ID thieves to steal your information. Just a quick glance is enough for you to see the scope of the problem:

- "Skimming" your credit cards at restaurants or stores
- Shoulder surfing your PIN at an ATM
- Picking up a bank deposit slip you used as scrap paper and threw away
- Hacking into your computer at home or at work
- Stealing your laptop or personal computer
- Sending you fake e-mails that trick you into releasing personal information
- Going through your garbage at home or at work
- Stealing your information from companies where you have accounts
- Stealing information while staying as a guest in your house

WHAT HAPPENS TO YOUR PERSONAL INFORMATION?

Personal information is a highly prized and very versatile commodity. Once a thief has your personal information, he or she can put it to all kinds of illegal uses — all of which can be extremely costly to you. Consider the following favorite activities of ID thieves:

- They get checks or debit cards made in your name and use them to empty your bank accounts.

- They take out loans or second mortgages in your name.

- They open new credit card accounts in your name. (Sometimes they use a mailing address other than yours, so it may take you weeks or months to realize that you have a problem.)

- They open a bank account in your name and write bad checks on the account.

- They establish Internet services in your name.

- They establish telephone or utility services in your name.

- They obtain automobile loans in your name.

- They use your stolen identity if they are arrested for a crime. When they do not appear for the court date, you could be arrested.

- They go on spending sprees using your credit and debit cards to buy "big ticket" items, such as computers, that they can easily sell.

- They file for bankruptcy under your name to avoid paying debts they have incurred using your identity.

- They use your identity in a marriage ceremony and use the marriage license to get immigration status in the country.

- They open accounts at a brokerage house and leave you liable for any losses.

- They use your social security number or social insurance number to get a job, leaving you liable for taxes due on that income.

- They could use your social security number or social insurance number to file a tax return and receive your refund.

No matter which one — or combination — of these crimes is committed against you, you will be left with the problem of clearing your name and rebuilding your credit rating, and you could also be left with a large debt load or a criminal record. Restoring your credit rating or removing incorrect criminal records can take months of letter writing, phone calls, and personal expense. Unfortunately, years later, the data could resurface, and you could become a victim again.

On November 30, 2005, the Internet Crime Complaint Center (IC3) issued the following warning:

ATTENTION — E-MAIL DISGUISED AS THE INTERNAL REVENUE SERVICE (IRS) PHISHING FOR PERSONAL INFORMATION

The FBI has become aware of a spam e-mail claiming the recipient is eligible to receive a tax refund for $571.94. The e-mail purports to be from tax-returns@irs.gov with the subject line of "IRS Tax Refund." A link is provided in the e-mail to access a form required to be completed in order to receive the refund. The link appears to connect to the true IRS website. However, the recipient is redirected to http://www.porterfam.org/2005/, where personal data, including credit card information, is captured.

THIS E-MAIL IS A HOAX. DO NOT FOLLOW THE PROVIDED LINK.

DETECTING IDENTITY THEFT

How would you know if your identity was stolen? In some cases, you may not discover it for months. However, there are early warning signs you should watch for:

- Your credit card statement or bank statement does not arrive in the mail as expected. (An identity thief may have submitted a change of address notice to your financial agency so you do not detect the charges he or she placed on your cards.)

- Your bank or credit card statement contains transactions that you did not authorize. (If this happens to you, check with your financial institution or lender immediately. Sometimes a thief will make a purchase for a few dollars to test your card. If the transaction is approved, he or she will immediately go on a large spending spree.)

- Your mail stops arriving. (The ID thief may have placed a change of address at the post office.)

- You receive credit card bills for unknown accounts. (The thief may have already applied for credit in your name.)

- You get a call from a collection agency for a debt you did not incur.

- You apply for credit from a lender and are unexpectedly denied it.

- You order your credit report and find accounts or debts listed that do not belong to you.

- A lender contacts you to discuss a credit application you did not submit.

- You receive a call or letter stating that you have been approved for or denied a loan by unknown creditors.

- You receive unknown utility or telephone statements in your name and address.

These are all indications of potential identity theft. If you notice any of them, you must immediately investigate the situation and take steps to correct it. By responding quickly, you stand a chance of controlling the damage.

HOW SAFE IS YOUR IDENTITY?

Protecting your personal information takes effort on your part. To understand how great your personal risk is, try taking the Identity Risk Test in Checklist 1. Each statement represents a possible risk factor. Read each statement carefully, and if you agree with it, check the box beside it. When you are finished the test, count up all the check marks and compare that number to the results shown in Table 1.

Checklist 1
Your Identity Risk Test

Question	Check
I don't order an annual credit report to check for fraud or mistakes.	
I carry my SSN or SIN card and other unnecessary cards in my wallet or purse.	
I don't crosscut shred banking and credit information when I throw it in the trash.	
I don't crosscut shred preapproved credit offers or convenience checks (from credit card companies) when I receive them.	
I don't believe people would root around in my trash looking for credit or financial information.	
I don't conceal personal information in my house from all relatives and visitors.	
My mail is delivered to an unsecured mailbox.	
My outgoing mail is put in an unsecured mailbox.	
I don't regularly update my software for security.	
I provide personal information whenever asked, without asking how it will be used or if it is necessary for me to divulge it.	
I don't check for people who might be listening when I give out information.	
My SSN or SIN is publicly displayed or used at work or school (for example, on timecards, receipts, or badges, etc.).	
When I enter my PIN, I don't cover it with my hand.	
I allow credit cards or other identification cards to remain in public sight when making purchases.	
I allow my credit cards to leave my sight when making a purchase.	
I might click on an e-mail link if the e-mail asks me to update my data at my bank or my favorite shopping sites.	
I have a listed phone number.	
I sometimes respond to Internet surveys or telephone solicitors.	
I keep my car registration papers in the glove box.	
I keep personal papers in my car.	
I don't have strong Internet protection software or hardware on my computer.	
I don't teach my children about computer security.	
I don't teach my children to keep personal information private when talking to strangers or friends.	
Total number of check marks	

Table 1
Identity Risk Test Results

Over 5 check marks	You are at high risk of ID theft.
1 to 5 check marks	You understand identity theft, but still need to do more to protect yourself and your family.
0 check marks	Congratulations. Keep up the good work!

HOW THIS BOOK CAN HELP YOU

By now you've probably realized that you must begin to think about and treat your personal information in an entirely different way than you have done until now. You have to protect it like you would a child. You have to keep it safe and establish control over who has access to it and how it can be used.

No longer will you gladly answer questions when credit grantors ask or automatically give personal data to retailers simply because they say they need to know. You will only release what is necessary — why they need to know. You will only release what is necessary — and no more. And you will demand they protect it from thieves, both inside and outside their companies, and make them explain their security precautions to your satisfaction.

This book will look at the ways you can protect your information so you never become a victim of identity theft. And if it is too late for you and your identity has already been stolen, this book will show you how to restore your reputation and your credit rating. It includes all the necessary contact numbers and forms to help you deal with the problems you will face.

Keep this book as a reference if you are not a victim and as a repair manual if you are.

In one notorious case of identity theft, the criminal, a convicted felon, not only incurred more than $100,000 of credit card debt, obtained a federal home loan, and bought homes, motorcycles, and handguns in the victim's name, but also called his victim to taunt him, saying that he could continue to pose as the victim for as long as he wanted because identity theft was not a federal crime at that time. The thief then filed for bankruptcy, also in the victim's name.

In this case, the victim reported he spent more than four years restoring his credit. It cost him more than $15,000.

2

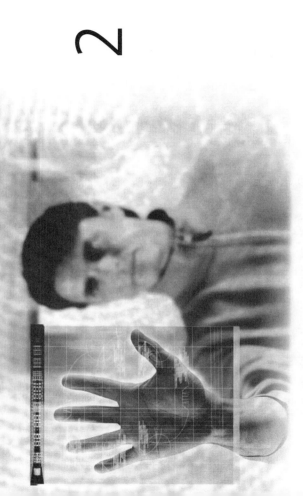

PREVENTING IDENTITY THEFT

When it comes to protecting your personal information, no one can do a better job than you can. After all, you can choose to grant or deny anyone access to it. And if you do choose to share your personal information, you can choose how much you want to divulge.

But as we discussed in the previous chapter, protecting your personal information requires a shift in your thinking. It also requires some effort. You need to be aware of the dangers in situations and circumstances you once thought commonplace.

This chapter discusses a number of everyday scenarios and what you can do to protect yourself in each one. The first thing to realize, however, is that you often *give* your information away.

WHEN YOU GIVE YOUR INFORMATION AWAY

Believe it or not, some information is not stolen. You simply give it away. For example, when you buy something in a store, the clerk may ask you for your phone number or address for the warranty.

Stores always have a variety of reasons to justify why they need the data, although in most cases, it is only for marketing purposes — not for your protection or benefit.

Think about all the people asking you for your personal information — the department store when you had that stove delivered, the time you took that computer course and they wanted your e-mail address, or the time you bought that book via the Internet. Everyone wants all kinds of data that they claim is "necessary" for them to have.

Unfortunately, once that information is out there, it does not go away. It becomes a valued asset of the company that acquired it and will continue to reside on that company's computer systems. As companies change owners or merge with other companies, your personal data gets copied over and over again. The companies that inherit your data often sell it to marketing firms, who in turn sell it to other companies. Data-mining companies will search for information across company networks and compile statistics and personal records on you. Everyone sees your personal information as an asset to be traded and used to make a profit.

Sometimes your personal data is accidentally circulated. For example, millions of faxes are sent each day. There have been cases where information has been faxed to the wrong number and personal financial data has been divulged.

This case was reported by the Office of the Privacy Commissioner of Canada.

"In late 2004, the Office of the Privacy Commissioner of Canada commenced an investigation into incidents involving misdirected facsimiles. These faxes, containing the personal information of customers of the Canadian Imperial Bank of Commerce (CIBC), were sent by various branches of the bank to a company in the United States and another in Dorval, Quebec.

"The incidents in question covered the period from 2001 to 2004. There were many commonalities between these incidents. In both cases, faxes were misdirected, and the recipients notified the bank repeatedly. While there was some evidence that the bank, specifically the Customer Care Centre and the legal branch, attempted to solve the problem, its efforts were ineffective. In 2002, the bank asked the US company to shred the misdirected faxes. Two years later, it learned that the company had not shredded everything. In 2004, when confronted with a Dorval business owner telling the bank that he was receiving facsimiles containing customer personal information, the bank nevertheless asked him to shred the misdirected faxes. In both cases, CIBC took no other measures to recover the personal information of its clients, and with the exception of one individual, the affected customers were not notified that their personal information had been faxed to the wrong location until after the matter became public in 2004."

Even government organizations may share your personal data with other government organizations.

However, just because someone asks you for personal information doesn't mean you have to let him or her have it, even if you are engaged in a commercial transaction with him or her. Whenever people ask for your personal information, stop and consider whether or not it is really necessary for them to have it. Ask them —

- why they need it,
- how it will be used,
- what happens to your personal data once you give it to them,
- how the company secures it to protect it from theft or misuse, and
- what will happen if you don't give it to them.

Most people will not be able to answer these questions. However, if they cannot, they have no right to your personal information in the first place.

If they do have answers for you, but you aren't happy with those answers, carefully consider whether or not the purchase is worth the trade of your personal information. Better yet, consider shopping at another store — one that *can* provide satisfactory answers.

In response to consumer concern over the treatment of personal information, many companies have developed privacy policies and also allow their customers to "opt out" if they wish, but privacy policies and opt-outs both have limitations. Read on to find out what they can — and can't — do for you.

How good is a company's privacy policy?

A privacy policy is simply a statement of the company's intention to protect your personal information and of the strict use to which they will put that information.

When dealing with a company, check its privacy policy before releasing any of your data. A strong privacy policy should clearly state —

- the company's purpose in collecting your data,
- that the collection of data is allowed only for that purpose,
- that the data will be used only for that purpose, and
- that the data will not be sold or redirected.

This policy should also tell you how the company will protect your information and allow you to see your complete record if you request it.

The US Financial Modernization Act of 1999 — also known as the Gramm-Leach-Bliley Act (GLB Act) — was designed to protect personal financial information held by financial institutions. A brief synopsis of the act can be found at www.ftc.gov/bcp/conline/pubs/buspubs /glbshort.htm.

The Federal Trade Commission is responsible for enforcing companies' privacy policies.

Unfortunately, even if a company has a strong policy, the strength of that policy is only as good as the company's weakest link. Often your information is stolen by hackers or is accidentally released by staff mistakes.

In addition, when a company goes bankrupt, many times the first thing the trustees sell is the client information. In this case, all the client records pass to the purchasing company, which may have a weak privacy policy. It might also sell your data to any number of marketing companies.

However, even if a company you're dealing with remains financially stable and the client records never change hands, no privacy policy can fully protect against the possibility of data being stolen by a staff member. In addition, database backup tapes can be lost, laptops containing client lists can be stolen, and hackers can sometimes access a company's records.

Table 2 shows just a few companies and organizations that have suffered data losses recently. Each of these companies had a strong privacy policy but was still unable to prevent the loss of data.

Total thefts of personal data have affected over 50 million Americans.

So how can you protect yourself? By treating your information as the valuable asset it is. Remember that it is not necessary to give out your personal information — certainly not for warranties or store purchases. If you buy something on the Internet, have it sent to a retail postal outlet instead of your home address. And if you must give a company an e-mail address, create a free temporary address and use that one.

There are many free providers of e-mail, such as www.hotmail .com or www.yahoo.com. Create an account for a few months, then cancel it and create a new one. And when you apply for a free e-mail account, protect yourself even further by not filling in accurate information such as your real name and address.

Remember that once you give your information away, you lose control over it and it can spread quickly to many places you do not want it to go. Each time someone new acquires your data, the chance it will be used for illegal purposes increases.

Table 2
Examples of Breach of Privacy

Company name	Type of breach	Number of people affected
ChoicePoint	Accessed by ID thieves	145,000
Time Warner	Lost backup tapes	600,000
Bank of America	Lost backup tape	1,200,000
Georgia DMV	Dishonest insider	Hundreds of thousands
Ameritrade	Lost backup tape	200,000
Wachovia, Bank of America, PNC Financial Services Group, and Commerce Bancorp	Dishonest insiders	676,000
Department of Justice	Stolen laptop	80,000
CitiFinancial	Lost backup tapes	3,900,000
CardSystems	Hacking	40,000,000
Georgia Southern University	Hacking	Tens of thousands

A synopsis of Canada's Personal Information Protection and Electronic Documents Act can be found at www.privcom.gc.ca/information /02_05_d_08_e.asp. Prepared by the Office of the Privacy Commission of Canada, the synopsis states, in part:

The law gives you the right to —

- know why an organization collects, uses, or discloses your personal information;

The law requires organizations to —

- obtain your consent when they collect, use or disclose your personal information;

- supply you with a product or a service even if you refuse consent for the collection, use or disclosure of your personal information unless that information is essential to the transaction;

- have personal information policies that are clear, understandable and readily available.

Opting out

Every piece of information you give a company is seen by them as an asset — something to be sold and traded. Fortunately, you often have the choice of opting out of companies dealing in your information. Many companies now offer you the opportunity to instruct them that they cannot use your personal information to market to you nor can they trade or sell your information to other organizations or individuals. In other words, you opt out. The more you opt out, the more control you retain over who has your information.

Unfortunately, opting out of every company that has access to your data can be tedious and time-consuming. Some companies require no more than a phone call from you. Others require a letter, and still others make it almost impossible for you to figure out how to opt out. Also, as many opt-outs expire after a certain period, you will have to go through the entire procedure again in a few years. Still, most companies do have an opt-out policy, and if possible, you should take advantage of it.

You should also consider getting an unlisted home telephone number. Once your telephone number and address are published in the telephone book, they are considered public information and can be used by marketing companies.

However, in the United States, the Telephone Consumer Protection Act states that telemarketers must maintain "do not call" lists. If you tell a company that you do not want to receive any more calls and they continue to call you, you can sue them for a small amount of money. Unfortunately, there is no central list of telemarketers, so you will have to inform each company individually.

You can also opt out of receiving direct-mail marketing from many national companies for five years by registering with the Direct Marketing Association's (DMA) Mail Preference Service.

To register with this service you can send a letter to —

Direct Marketing Association
Mail Preference Service
PO Box 643
Carmel, NY 10512

Or register online at www.dmaconsumers.org/offmailinglist.html. However, registering with the Mail Preference Service will stop mailings only from organizations that are registered with this service.

To use this service you must complete an online form at https://cornerstonewebmedia.com/cma/submit.asp. This service is valid only for member companies of the CMA and is good only for three years. For the opt-out to remain valid, you must continue to register your name.

In Canada, the Canadian Marketing Association (CMA) offers the Do Not Contact Service. It allows you to reduce the number of marketing offers you receive by mail, telephone, and fax.

Many people also find that deceased family members or friends receive mail solicitations. In the United States, you can now register the names of deceased loved ones with a new service through the Direct Marketing Association — the Deceased Do Not Contact List (DDNC).

To use this service, go to the DMA's website at https://preference.the-dma.org/cgi/ddnc.php. There is a $1 credit card verification fee to complete the registration. This fee helps to prevent fraudulent entries, as the DMA records names of those who are registering deceased loved ones.

THREATS AT WORK

You may believe your workplace is relatively safe, but you should think again. Your employer has a large amount of information on you and your family. Not only does your employer have your name, address, and telephone number on file, it may also keep a record, for insurance-benefit purposes, of the names and birth dates of all your immediate family members. It could retain information on personal addresses and contact phone numbers for emergencies. Of course, all employers will keep a record of your social security number (SSN) (or in Canada, your social insurance number (SIN)). Finally, your employer may have a digital copy of your résumé file — which would list your complete work and educational history.

All this data is highly sensitive. Your employer has a responsibility to see that it is handled with care and confidentiality, but it is also your responsibility to ensure that they do so.

Fortunately, there are a number of strategies both you and your employer can adopt to help ensure that your personal information is more secure in the workplace.

What your employer can do to protect your information

ID thefts from companies are often committed from inside — a staff member steals the data. Your employer should have a strict policy on who has access to personal information. Only a minimum of authorized personnel should be able to see any staff records. Even the computer services department should be allowed access only to such information as they require to perform their jobs.

A lost or stolen laptop or a stolen computer could contain thousands of personal records of clients or staff, so all laptops and computers at work should have their data encrypted and be physically secured — attached to the desk by security cables. Internal theft of unsecured laptops in particular is very common. Personal device assistants (PDAs) should also be treated with the same care and locked in a safe location when not in use. These devices are often synchronized with a desktop computer and can contain a great deal of data.

Your employer should also ensure that all paper records are cross-shredded on-site. Thieves will sometimes go "dumpster diving" through the company trash. In one case, a thief simply threw unattended recycling bins in his truck and drove off.

Your employer should also ensure that human resources staff do not leave printouts of personal data on their desks or on the printer any longer than is strictly necessary. Any staff member can walk by and see the data or steal it.

Your company should have policies in place to protect your data at work. For instance, your employer could institute a mandatory security-training course for staff and follow it up with regular reminders that information needs to be protected.

What you can do to protect your information

When it comes to protecting personal information in the workplace, you have an important role to play. First of all, ask your employer what procedures are already in place to guard personnel records. Feel free to suggest that the employer adopt any or all of the strategies discussed above.

Be aware that your coworkers may not all be completely trustworthy. Don't leave your purse or wallet unattended at work. It is very easy for someone to pick it up. They may not steal it, but may instead record your credit card information or other personal data and put it back before you notice.

If any strangers are walking unescorted around your office, ask them for an identification badge or other proof that they work for the company they say they do. If they cannot supply valid ID, call the company they represent to verify they work there and are supposed to be at your office. The person may be wearing a telephone company uniform, but that is not proof that they are from the telephone company. There have been recent cases of national courier company uniforms being sold on eBay. A uniform and a clipboard are not sufficient identification. That person could be a thief, on the premises to steal purses or laptops.

When you go on vacation, do not set up automatic e-mail replies that inform anyone sending you a message that you are away from the office. It also alerts them to the fact that your house could be empty until you return.

If your wallet or PDA was lost or stolen at work, notify both the human resources and security departments. You might recommend posting a notice warning other personnel to take additional security precautions. For example, do not store wallets or purses in unlocked desk drawers.

Never leave personal documents at work overnight, even in locked desk drawers. Many people, such as janitors or security guards, could have access to your office after work.

SHOPPING SECURELY

It's easy to fall into a friendly conversation in a store with a sales clerk, but you must think before you speak. Be cautious and make certain that conversation doesn't lead you into revealing personal details.

For instance, you should not mention where you work (and children should never reveal where they go to school). And don't talk about the reason for the purchase. Let's say you're buying a computer for your home. Don't mention that you're going to use it to connect to your workplace. A sales clerk could leverage enough information from you about the type of operating systems and networks you have at work to initiate a successful computer system attack. Many hackers use this kind of "social engineering" to get information before they start hacking into systems.

Should you find yourself in a casual conversation in a store, don't mention that you are going on holidays for three weeks starting Saturday and that's why you need the product right now. It indicates that your house could be empty and therefore an easy target. If a clerk manages to get your phone number, he or she can look up your address and break in while you are away.

It is very important to protect your personal information when shopping. The stores you shop at may feel a strong responsibility to protect your data, but the clerk processing your purchase may not feel that protecting your personal information is important. Even worse, as discussed above, he or she could be an identity thief. Therefore, release only information that is absolutely necessary to complete a transaction — such as your credit card number — not your phone numbers or address.

If you use a debit card to make a purchase, use your hand to hide the PIN as you enter it. It is easy for a thief to "shoulder surf" your PIN, then later steal your cards.

Be very aware of where you place any card. Do not leave it on the counter for even a moment. Cell phones with cameras are a popular way to get information from credit cards or driver's licenses left in public view. Very few people suspect a person holding or pretending to dial a cell phone, but someone standing near you who appears to be on his or her cell phone could be taking a picture of your card with the cell phone's camera. Or he or she might click a picture just by holding the cell casually near the card.

Never let a credit card leave your sight. There is no reason for a clerk to take it into the back room or do anything under the counter with it. This is a common way to get a copy of your card information. And whenever you get your card back, verify that it is yours.

Never leave your receipts behind. Some receipts show your entire credit or debit card number. If you do business with a store that prints the entire number on the receipt, tell them to change their systems so most of the number is not printed. If they can't accommodate your request, consider shopping elsewhere.

Choose a PIN that is unique. Don't use your birth date, part of your SSN or SIN, or other obvious number combinations such as 1111.

Change your PIN frequently — at least once a month. A good way to remember to do this is to time it with something you do every month. For example, every time you pay a certain bill, change your PIN.

Never write down your PIN in your checkbook or on your cards. Always memorize it rather than writing it down. If a thief steals your wallet or purse and it contained your PIN, you may not be reimbursed for money stolen from your accounts. In a situation such as this, many financial institutions hold you liable because you failed to protect your PIN.

ATM Scam

Thieves use a number of techniques to steal money from ATMs, but this one is a favorite.

Unnoticed by you, thieves will drop a $20 bill on the ground just behind you. Then they watch as you enter your PIN. As you wait for the ATM to release your card, they ask you if the money on the ground is yours. When you bend over to pick it up, they swap the card in the ATM slot with a fake card. They know it is unlikely that you'll check the card to ensure it is yours.

They have the timing down perfectly, and now they have not only your PIN, but also your card.

After you leave, they withdraw as much money as possible.

CHECK WASHING

Paying by check is no longer as safe as it used to be. The ink on checks can be "washed" and the information changed — which means it could be cashed by someone you did not designate and for much more money than you intended.

When a thief "washes" a check, he or she simply erases the ink with chemicals found in common household cleaning products. Then the thief rewrites the check in his or her own name, increasing the amount payable by hundreds and even thousands of dollars. It is estimated that Americans lose $815 million dollars a year to check washing.

If you do use checks, use a pen that embeds the ink in the paper and prevents washing of the ink. A number of manufacturers sell such pens. Uni-ball sells a pen called the "207" for about two dollars. It uses a gel ink that contains particles of color that become trapped in the paper, making check washing a lot more difficult.

Always use a credit or debit card for purchases. Unlike cash, cards will leave a trail of the transaction and some offer warranty protection.

COMPUTER PROTECTION

Hackers attack thousands of computers every day. It isn't just large corporate systems that are targets; it's individual home computers, too. Think about your own computer. It probably contains financial and personal information — your online banking data or personal details in e-mails or letters that a thief could use to steal your identity.

There are a number of ways for hackers to attack your computer, but luckily there are things you can do to make your computer more secure.

Guard your laptop

Thousands of laptops are stolen or misplaced every year in North America. They can be taken in airports, from cars, from workplaces, and from anywhere else you might carry one. In some airports, the security screeners have even stolen laptops.

Many people don't realize that the thief is often more interested in the data contained by the laptop than the laptop itself.

You need to guard your laptop, and the best way to protect the data on it is to prevent it from being stolen. Keep your laptop in the trunk of your car instead of the back seat, and use a locking device to attach it to the lid of the trunk.

At work, use a lock to attach your laptop to your desk. There are many reports of laptops being stolen from offices. There have been cases of staff members stealing a coworker's computer. Even at home, you should consider locking your computer to a solid piece of furniture. Sometimes thieves are in a hurry to leave and won't try to free a physically secured laptop.

At airports or coffee shops, don't place your laptop down beside you while sitting or getting your ticket or a coffee. That's more than enough time for a thief to steal it. Consider purchasing a proximity device that attaches to your laptop. It sounds a loud alarm if it is moved more than a few feet from a device in your pocket. Not only does it prevent theft, it also ensures that you'll never absentmindedly leave your laptop behind!

When you're in an airport or at any other transportation hub, always lock your laptop case. It not only prevents theft of the laptop from the case, but it also prevents anyone from putting anything into your case without you knowing it.

When you are traveling, don't carry your laptop in an expensive case with the computer's name blazoned across the front. Fool thieves into thinking you're carrying nothing valuable by using a style of carrying case that could contain clothes or personal effects.

You could also purchase encryption software to protect your data. These programs are simple to use and install, and can be purchased at most computer stores or online. If your laptop is stolen, an encryption program adds a strong layer of protection.

You can also make accessing your data much more difficult by using login passwords and other protection schemes, such as small biometric hardware devices that store your fingerprints in an internal database, then require you to login by placing your finger on a built-in or attachable reader. Some new laptops even have fingerprint readers built into the keyboard.

You can also purchase software programs that emit a signal when the thief uses your computer online. The software company's monitoring center will notify the local police of the laptop's location and even provide them with a map.

You should also think about purchasing a flash drive. These are small hard drives about the size of your thumb that can store large amounts of data. You could keep all important information on this drive instead of your laptop drive. The flash drive can be carried in your pocket away from your computer. You must be careful, however, not to misplace your flash drive. As an added protection measure, some flash drives now require your fingerprint to access the data.

You might think it inconvenient to take these safety measures, but when you consider the damage that could happen to you or your family as a result of stolen data, the steps described here are well worth it.

Secure your wireless connections

Many computers have wireless connection capabilities. A wireless connection allows a computer or laptop to connect to the Internet or a company network without physical cables — similar to how a cell phone works. Making a wireless connection secure is now very convenient, but most people don't bother, and attacks on wireless connections are on the rise.

Wireless signals leak far beyond the confines of your front door. Hackers can park near your house with a laptop loaded with detection software and gain immediate access to your unprotected system. This method of attack is called "war driving." Once they take over your computer, they can steal any data you have on it or use it to store illegal files or pictures for later retrieval. You will not be aware of the files, but you could be nonetheless held liable by the police if they are found on your system. Hackers could also use your computer to hack into others, and the trail would lead back to you.

Away from home, many airports, hotels, and coffee shops now offer wireless connections. Unfortunately, these connections may also lack any type of security. That person sitting across the room with a laptop could easily be accessing your system.

Wireless connections can be secured, however. If necessary, ask an experienced computer professional for help to ensure your wireless software has all its security options properly set. Often, the store where you made the purchase will have a staff member or contact that could assist you. Ensure that this person is bonded and is well known to the store. Be careful hiring someone out of a newspaper ad as he or she could be an identity thief.

At the same time, make certain that you've secured your BlackBerry connection and/or that PDA with its wireless e-mail capabilities.

Keep safe on the Internet

The Internet is not only a necessity for many people, but also a fount of knowledge and fun. And anything that's that much fun should be enjoyed to the fullest.

Unfortunately, the Internet is also one of the most popular places for thieves to steal information. For example, they could send you an e-mail with an attachment. The e-mail can be made to look like it comes from a friend or a trusted company — quite harmless. However, a sender's e-mail address can be faked, and the attachment could be a program written to steal data or give thieves illegal access to your computer without you knowing it. If you open the attachment, they could have free and full use of your computer.

Hacking is another common problem. There are programs on the Internet that continuously search for unprotected computers. If one is found, the computer address is sent back to the thieves for use later in an attack.

Or attackers could try to trick you into releasing your information. They send you an e-mail saying you can buy current software for ridiculously low prices. Should you visit their website and fill in your credit card information, the software never arrives. It's just a scam to get your credit card number.

Sometimes the people trying to get information from you are marketing companies. When you visit their website, they secretly place a small program on your computer called a "cookie." The cookie doesn't harm your computer but is designed to track all the sites you visit on the web. The data is eventually sent back to the marketing firm so they can build a profile of your habits and send targeted advertising to your computer.

These tactics range from merely deceptive to truly ingenious, but you can protect yourself.

First, buy Internet protection software for your computer. This software can protect your computer from viruses, from hackers trying to break into your computer — and from spyware.

Spyware programs monitor your computer activity and send the data to the computer of the person or organization using the program. Among the information that may be transmitted are passwords, login details, account numbers, personal information, individual files, or other personal documents.

Without being aware of it, you can pick up spyware from websites, e-mail messages, and instant messengers. You can also end up with spyware on your computer simply because you installed a free downloaded software program.

There are a number of excellent programs available in computer stores or online that exist just to lock your computer door. They will stop viruses from attacking your computer, they can prevent hackers from attempting to break into your computer, and they can prevent spyware from being installed.

For example, programs such as Norton Internet Security and McAfee Internet Security are designed to protect you online. They automatically update themselves to protect you against the latest threats. Once again, a trusted computer professional can assist you in choosing an appropriate product.

However, one product won't be enough to protect you from all threats. (In the software industry, one is never enough.) Although these products protect you against most attacks and viruses, no single software protects you against everything. For instance, you'll not only need a program to protect you against spyware, but also another for cookies because Internet protection software is not designed to block or remove cookies from your computer.

The list below mentions types of programs you can use to protect your computer and gives names of examples.

However, I don't recommend any particular product. There is no "best" product. All have their own strengths and weaknesses, and your needs will vary depending on how you use your computer and what you use it for. Ask a trusted computer security professional for advice on what software is best for your particular situation.

Internet security software

Internet security software is designed to protect you against someone accessing your computer while you are online. It can protect you against hackers trying to steal your personal information. (For more information on hackers, see the section "Hackers" later on in this chapter.) Many of these programs also provide protection against viruses, spyware, and spam. Two popular brands are Norton Internet Security and McAfee Internet Security Suite.

Parental-control software

Parental-control software allows you to monitor what your child is doing on the web. For instance, you can set the software to prevent personal information from being sent over the computer. A child may release information that you feel is personal in a chatroom or in an e-mail, such as your address or that you are going on holidays and your house will be empty. This software can also detect viruses in files your child downloads — which can be useful, as viruses are often attached to free music and game file downloads. (For more information on children and identity theft, see the section "What Your Children Need to Know.")

Anti-virus software

Computer viruses can destroy data on your computer or steal personal information. Anti-virus software protects your computer against viruses embedded in e-mails or downloaded files.

Anti-spyware software

Some spyware programs record the websites you visit and can record your login information. Some can even steal information on your computer. Anti-spyware software prevents your computer from picking up programs that record what you do on the web.

There are some free programs available for download from the web. For example, Microsoft currently offers a free anti-spyware program on their website. However, these programs are single-purpose systems. They may block spyware, but will not stop viruses or hacking.

Just as a car requires maintenance, so does a computer. But once you've put proper protection in place, the fun can start again.

Still, there are methods thieves use to steal data that no software can protect against. These methods attack a computer's "wet wear" — its human user. Here's how they work, and how you can defend yourself.

Watch for phishing scams

Some attacks are not on the computer, but on the computer user instead. A very popular way of attacking the user is "phishing" (pronounced "fishing"). It's become one of the fastest-growing methods of stealing data today.

Phishing is a kind of e-mail con game. The idea is to trick you into actually giving away your personal information. Thieves send out millions of phishing e-mails in the hope that they can "catch" a few unsuspecting users. A sample e-mail is shown below.

SAMPLE PHISHING E-MAIL

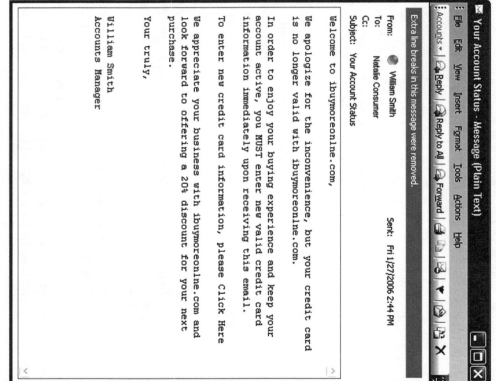

Your Account Status - Message (Plain Text)

File   Edit   View   Insert   Format   Tools   Actions   Help

Accounts ▾ | Reply | Reply to All | Forward |

Extra line breaks in this message were removed.

From: ● William Smith
To: Natalie Consumer
Cc:
Subject: Your Account Status

Sent: Fri 1/27/2006 2:44 PM

Welcome to ibuymoreonline.com,

We apologize for the inconvenience, but your credit card is no longer valid with ibuymoreonline.com.

In order to enjoy your buying experience and keep your account active, you MUST enter new valid credit card information immediately upon receiving this email.

To enter new credit card information, please Click Here

We appreciate your business with ibuymoreonline.com and look forward to offering a 20% discount for your next purchase.

Your truly,

William Smith
Accounts Manager

This is how it works:

You receive an e-mail that is forged to look like it's from a legitimate company, such as eBay or a bank. The e-mail urges you to update your personal information immediately, such as passwords and credit card numbers, often telling you that your account will be closed or canceled if you do not. These e-mails always contain a link for you to click to complete the update. When you click it, you are taken to a website that seems to belong to the company or bank.

Unfortunately, that site is a fake designed to appear as if it were genuine. It may even display forged logos to enhance the appearance of legitimacy. Instead, it is owned and operated by the thief. If you fill in your information and click "submit," your data is sent straight to the thief. Your browser is then directed to the real company's site so that you don't suspect a thing.

By sending out large numbers of these e-mails, the "phisher" can count on a certain percentage of the recipients being "hooked" into entering their information. In one phishing scam in which the e-mails were forged to look as if they came from a bank, more than 40 percent of the recipients responded.

Phishing Growth

Microsoft attorney Aaron Kornblum recently reported, "Phishers are thieves, and thieves in the online world, as in the real world, are working very hard to separate personal financial information and other data from their victims."

The software maker recently filed 117 lawsuits against alleged operators of phishing websites — a major step forward in thwarting online criminals, according to Kornblum.

However, he acknowledged that there may be as much to fear in the future from phishing as there is to learn from its past.

"People will continue to think up new ways to apply phishing techniques and deceive consumers," he said. "The sophistication is growing, and it's not that surprising at all."

Phishing is growing in Canada, too, but many consumers are not aware of it. According to a recent Canadian survey on phishing, Visa Canada reported that the majority of people with an e-mail address and Internet access have never heard of phishing, despite a global 50 percent monthly increase in phishing incidents.

Visa, the Royal Canadian Mounted Police (RCMP), and the Competition Bureau joined forces to declare November 3rd "Anti-Phishing Day" and launched a consumer-awareness campaign to help inform Canadians about phishing scams.

On average, a consumer loses $1,200 when his bank account is taken over.

This is escalating into such a problem for banks that many of them now refuse to protect their customers. Instead they are choosing to "litigate, fight, and force consumers to settle for lower amounts."

There are ways to detect when an e-mail could be fraudulent.

Watch your cursor when you point it at a link in an e-mail. If it changes to a hand shape, that's a good indication that the link is not text — a sign that the e-mail itself could be a scam. Phishers will create the website link as a picture. It will look like a proper site address, such as "accounts@ebay.com," but is actually a picture of the words. Behind that picture is the attackers' site address. When you click it, it redirects you to the attackers' website, which is designed to look like the legitimate one. You'll think you're entering your updated data into the legitimate site, but instead you're sending it directly to the thief.

There may be other signs that the e-mail is not legitimate. Look for obvious spelling and grammatical errors. Many phishing schemes originate from outside North America, and the authors are not always fluent in English.

Don't trust an e-mail simply because you believe you know the sender. A sender's address can be faked, so an e-mail can be made to appear as if it's coming from anyone. It is highly unlikely a company will send an e-mail requesting your personal information. If you want to confirm any request made of you by e-mail, contact the sender by phone, or type the website address given in the e-mail into your browser. Never copy and paste it from the e-mail.

If you decide to click a link to a website, take note of the address on the website first. Most legitimate sites will have a relatively short address, such as www.ebay.com. Fraudulent sites are more likely to have a long string of characters in the name, with the legitimate business name appearing somewhere in the string or possibly not at all.

Fraudsters also buy website names that are very similar to the real website name. For example, they may buy the website name www.banksofamerica.com when the real name of the legitimate organization's website is www.bankofamerica.com. If a user types an "s" into the name, his or her browser opens a fake site that looks like the original.

If you type a website address into your browser, look for indicators that the site is secure, such as a lock icon 🔒 in the lower right corner of the browser's status bar. If you double-click on the icon, you'll see the site's certificate information, indicating the identity of the remote computer.

Ensure the website's address starts with "https" rather than "http." The "s" stands for secure. For example, https://www.mybank.com/balances.htm is a secure page, but http://www.mybank.com/balances.htm is not.

These signs do not constitute absolute assurance that the site is secure, but they are certainly good indications of it.

To help keep yourself safe, don't send personal information in any e-mail. No e-mail is confidential, even at work. If you are not willing to yell something out on the street corner, don't put it in an e-mail.

Protect yourself during online transactions

Use a credit card for transactions on the Internet. If someone compromises your credit card, your personal liability is limited. For added security, many banks now offer single-use low-limit credit cards that expire within one or two months.

Use just one credit card for all online purchases. It makes it much easier to track your transactions.

Do not respond to Internet offers that sell products for large reductions in price. For example, it is common to see software offered for sale at large discounts. The problem is, you may never receive the software. Often these offers conceal a fraud scheme aimed at getting your personal and credit card information.

Hackers

Hackers today do not really need to know a great deal about computers to gain access to your system. There are hundreds of hacking programs available for free on the Internet, and most are very simple to use. There are also websites devoted to hackers helping one another learn how to attack computers.

The following tips can help you keep your personal information safe on your computer:

- Use an Internet protection software program (such as Norton Internet Security) that prevents intruders from accessing your computer via the Internet. You could also use a hardware device that blocks hackers. Many routers act as hardware firewalls to offer additional protection. A combination of both software and hardware protection is ideal. There are a number of books or professionals that can help you with your choices. Perhaps one of your larger computer retail stores could recommend a consultant. Do not operate a computer on the Internet without some sort of protection.

- Install and maintain virus-protection software. Most protection software can be set to update itself automatically. Computer viruses can have a variety of damaging effects, including allowing outsiders access to your files or other stored information.

- Keep all your software programs up to date with the latest patches. Unfortunately, most software programs are released to the market before all the bugs have been worked out. As the public begins to complain about the problems, the makers issue patches to fix the problems. To ensure you have the latest security fixes, always keep up to date with the newest patches. They can be downloaded at each software company's website. For instance, to update Internet Explorer, visit www.microsoft.com.

- Be cautious about opening attachments to any e-mails, regardless of who sent them. It is easy to make an e-mail appear as if it were from a friend. Simply opening a file could expose your system to a computer Trojan — a program that can steal any personal information stored on your computer.

- Make certain you have the most recent version of your web browser. Newer browsers will contain the latest security updates to prevent attacks on your computer and guard your online transactions.

- If you store financial information on your laptop, use a strong access password such as a combination of letters (upper- and lowercase), numbers, and symbols. For example, instead of "traveler" use "Tr2Ve$er."

- Don't use an automatic login feature that saves your user name and password so you don't have to enter them each time you log in to a site, and when you are finished, always log off. That way, if your laptop is stolen, it's harder for the thief to access your personal information.

PDAs (Personal digital assistants)

Your Palm Pilot or other handheld PDA device contains a wealth of information about you and your friends, and all of it could increase the risk of identity theft should it get into the wrong hands.

Protect your PDA by purchasing a password protection program so that if an unauthorized user turns on your PDA, only a login screen will appear. Most password products range in features and are priced from $10 to $30. Some of the more advanced products offer data encryption, while others simply offer a password on start-up, leaving the data in the device unencrypted. You can also engrave the back of the PDA with a mailbox address and offer a reward for its return.

Discard your computer with care

Now that you're protecting your data, it's even more important to ensure you destroy it when you discard or recycle your computers. This includes cell phones, fax machines, and your PDAs. Even company photocopiers now have hard drives that could contain important information.

Before you give away or dispose of a computer, destroy all the data on it. Don't rely on simply deleting information to get rid of it. In most cases, the information remains recoverable for someone with the right tools and knowledge.

It takes specialized software to ensure the data is completely unrecoverable. Get yourself a "wiping" utility program and overwrite the entire hard drive. If you're still concerned, remove the hard drive and physically destroy it. Be sure you do the same with CDs and floppy disks that contain information you don't want to keep. Many shredders will destroy computer media.

Ensure you also destroy data in cell phones, PDAs, fax machines, and other electronic devices before discarding or recycling them.

Burning any computer media, such as CDs, can release dangerous toxins that could cause damage to your health. If you want to discard computer media, locate a local company that can guarantee complete certified destruction for you.

WHAT YOUR CHILDREN NEED TO KNOW

It is very important to educate your children about all kinds of dangers in the world today. They need to be aware of not only the physical dangers, but also the danger of giving away too much family information.

Start by keeping your financial information private from your children, and do not allow them access to your credit cards. Talk to them about what things must be kept confidential — and why.

Children's friends

An adult will not talk about personal information such as bank accounts and credit card data, even with trusted friends and relatives. However, a child might not understand the importance of keeping these things confidential.

Teach your children what personal information is and that they should never release it — even to a friend or relative — without first asking a parent or guardian for permission.

Children and the Internet

It is important to educate your children about the dangers of the Internet. For example, you may see an e-mail and recognize it as a scam. However, a child may receive a fabulous offer for a game or music download and be tricked into entering a parent's charge card number to get it. The site could also request names, personal addresses, or birth dates. A child may not know that they do not need to give out this information. There have also been cases where a child has used a parent's credit card to gamble online. In such cases, the parents are liable for all losses.

Many children use the Internet to download free music and games. Hackers often offer this type of free software in the hope that children will download and install it. Unfortunately, these downloads could contain programs designed to steal personal information from your computer. Although protection software will block this type of attack, some children will disable the software to continue the download.

Chatrooms can also be dangerous for children. A child will sometimes discuss things that an adult knows is personal. They may discuss where you work or where you bank. They may even mention that the family is going on holidays for a couple of weeks, which means your house will be unattended.

A large number of websites are available to help you teach your children about Internet safety. Should you or your child visit these sites, do not complete any optional surveys or release any personal data, such as your e-mail address. It is always best to surf the web anonymously.

For more information about protecting your children on the Internet, see *Protect Your Child on the Internet: A Parent's Toolkit*, also published by Self-Counsel Press.

PROTECTING YOUR HOME

Your home is a perfect place for identity thieves to steal your personal information. Thieves often break into your house only to steal your personal information, which can bring them more money than your stereo or television would.

The most common trouble spots are your mailbox, trash, and telephone. We'll discuss each and what you can do to protect yourself.

Mail

Your mail contains all kinds of personal information about you, and thieves can easily plunder it. Incoming mail, outgoing mail, and mail you throw away are all favorite targets.

Never use an unlocked postal box. Always empty your mailbox promptly.

Deposit outgoing mail in post-office collection boxes or at your local post office instead of in an unsecured mailbox.

If you're planning to be away from home and can't pick up your mail, call the post office to ask for a vacation hold or have your mail redirected while you are away. American readers should contact their local post office to have this done. Canadian readers have the option of using Canada Post's website to stop mail delivery while on vacation: www.canadapost.ca/personal /offerings/supplementary_services_pers/can/hold-e.asp.

If you notice that you've suddenly stopped receiving mail, check immediately with the post office. Some ID thieves will complete a change-of-address form to divert your mail to another location. They retrieve it from there and harvest your personal information from it.

Guard outgoing mail. As mentioned earlier, a thief can take your checks and "wash" the ink. They can then rewrite your checks for larger amounts and make them payable to themselves.

Trash

Your garbage can be a treasure trove for identity thieves who go dumpster diving to steal personal information. Thieves will sometimes sort through your trash in the hope of finding financial statements or receipts that show credit card numbers.

Thwart them by shredding your charge receipts, copies of credit applications or offers, check and bank statements, expired credit cards, etc. Keep a crosscut shredder in your home and use it often. Many crosscut shredders also destroy credit cards and computer media.

Any piece of paper in your home could contain personal information. Ensure you properly destroy all records — even personal notes.

Teach your children to be very careful of what they throw away.

Guard your deposit slips. A thief would much rather have one of your deposit slips than a blank check. Using that deposit slip, they will make a large deposit into your account using a check that they know will bounce. On the deposit slip they will include a cash withdrawal for a lesser amount. By the time the check is returned marked insufficient funds, they are long gone. Don't use your deposit slips as scratch paper and then throw them away.

Telephone

Don't give out personal information on the phone unless you've initiated the contact or personally know the person with whom you are talking. Identity thieves may pose as the representatives of banks, Internet service providers (ISPs), or even government agencies to get you to reveal identity information.

Before you divulge any personal information, confirm that you're dealing with a legitimate representative from a real organization. Call customer service using the number on your account statement or from the telephone book. Describe the phone call you've just received and ask if it's valid.

On September 28, 2005, the FBI National Press Office in Washington, DC, warned the public against a scheme involving jury service.

They stated that individuals identifying themselves as US court employees were telephoning citizens and telling them they'd been selected for jury duty. They then asked for social security numbers and credit card numbers. If the citizens refused to divulge the information, they were threatened with fines.

The press office emphasized that the judicial system does not contact people by phone and ask for personal information such as a social security number, date of birth, or credit card numbers.

CREDIT AND DEBIT CARDS

Before revealing any identifying information on any application form, ask how the data is used and whether it will be shared with any other company or organization. If your personal information is stolen from your credit card company, it may reimburse you for its card but will not help you if your data is used to acquire other loans.

Limit the number of credit and debit cards that you carry to what you actually need.

At home, be sure to safeguard credit information. Store it where roommates, outside help, or service workers can't see it.

Place passwords on your credit cards and bank cards. Avoid using an obvious password such as your mother's maiden name or your birth date or phone number, or a series of consecutive numbers. Maximize your protection by using different passwords for each account.

Review credit card and bank account statements as soon as you receive them to determine whether there are any unauthorized charges. Immediately ask your bank or lender about any charges you don't recognize.

Photocopy your cards (both sides) or make a list of the names, account numbers, and expiration dates of your cards, as well as the contact phone numbers printed on the back, and keep these records in a safe place in case your cards are lost or stolen and you need to alert your credit card companies. I always keep a photocopy of all my identification and credit cards in a safety deposit box.

As well as signing your credit cards, write "PHOTO ID REQUIRED" on the backs.

When you are writing checks to pay your credit card accounts, do not write the full credit card number on the check. Use only the last four numbers. The credit card company knows the rest of the number.

CAR RISKS

Your car usually contains very important personal information. The laws of most countries require you to carry your vehicle registration and insurance in the car. These papers show your name and address, and could include financial data such as where your car was financed.

Many people also keep a garage-door opener in their cars. Combined with your address, this device gives a thief easy access to your house.

You can do little about the registration papers unless you carry them with you, which is very impractical. However, for some additional protection, you could keep them in the trunk.

As for the garage-door opener, never leave it in plain sight on your visor or your dashboard. You can now purchase door openers that fit on a key chain.

If your car is stolen or broken into, immediately change the code on your garage door.

Never leave personal papers in your car, including mail, receipts, or any document that contains personal information.

Never leave your laptop in your car. You may be running into the store for just a few seconds to pick up something, but most car thieves can steal a car faster than you can buy your milk.

THE THREAT YOU CARRY

One of the most common ways thieves steal your ID is by stealing your wallet or purse. People often carry more cards than they need for day-to-day living. Take a good look at all the cards you normally carry and ask yourself if you need to have them with you at all times. If not, leave those cards at home in a safe.

Make a list of what you do carry in your wallet or purse. If your wallet or purse is stolen, you'll know whom to contact to get those cards replaced.

A photocopy of these cards works even better. Ensure that you photocopy the front and back of each card.

Keep the photocopy or list in a safe place at home or in a location you can access easily in case of a theft. If your wallet or purse is stolen on a weekend, you will need to call the credit card companies immediately. If you keep the list in a safety deposit box in a bank, make certain the bank is one you can access outside normal working hours.

Use Checklist 2 to record the details of your identification.

If any of these cards also contain your social insurance number or social security number, note that down.

ON VACATION AND STILL AT RISK

Identity theft can happen on vacation as well as at home, so you must also guard your personal information when you're traveling. It is just as important to protect any receipts you receive, such as those from the hotel or car rental agency, as it is to protect your personal belongings. Keep all receipts with you and do not discard anything unless you can destroy it properly.

Checklist 2
Identification Document Checklist

Record every card you carry in your wallet or purse in case of theft. Keep this document in a safe place for reference.

Item	Record any numbers or details on the item
Driver's license	
Credit cards:	
Visa	
MasterCard	
American Express	
Other	
ATM card	
Debit card	
Check-cashing card	
Bank checks	
SSN/SIN	
Auto insurance card	
Medicare or Medi-Cal card	
Health insurance/prescription/dental benefit cards	
Employee or student ID card	
Military ID card	
Green card or immigration papers	
Passport	
Long-distance calling card	
Prepaid phone cards	
Birth certificate	
Store club cards (Costco, etc.)	
Professional licenses	
Personal address book	
Codes, passwords, or authorization information	
Other	

Do not carry a wallet or purse while on vacation. Use a concealed money belt.

If you have to leave any identification in a hotel room, always use the room's safe. If the room has none, you can give it to reception to keep in the hotel safe. Take some precautions, though. There's always the possibility that the hotel staff may steal your information. Put your ID in a sealed envelope and sign across the seal before you give it to reception for safekeeping. You will know if someone opens the envelope because the seal — and your signature — will be broken.

Use strong entry passwords on any laptop you bring with you and secure it to a fixed piece of furniture.

Before you leave home, give a photocopy or list of all credit cards, licenses, and any other identification to a relative or friend whom you trust implicitly. If your wallet or purse is stolen, you can contact that person for a copy of the information. However, remember that relatives can commit identity thefts too, so choose wisely.

Make sure your list includes the required phone numbers for reporting any theft. Do not have the list faxed to a hotel or any other location. Where you have an Internet connection, an encrypted e-mail is a safe method of getting the list. If you are traveling in a country that does not allow easy contact with your relative or friend but which has branch offices of your credit card companies, carry a copy of the list, but do not keep it in your purse or wallet, and guard it well.

Don't tell everyone you are going on vacation. You really don't want everyone to know that your house will be left unattended.

THE DANGER CARD (SSN/SIN)

In the United States, each citizen has a social security number (SSN). The SSN was created in 1936 as a nine-digit account number assigned by the Secretary of Health and Human Services for the purpose of administering the social security laws. SSNs were first intended for use exclusively by the federal government as a means of tracking earnings to determine the amount of social security taxes to credit to each worker's account. In 1961, Congress authorized the Internal Revenue Service (IRS) to use SSNs as taxpayer identification numbers.

In 1974, Congress passed the Privacy Act, which among other things, makes it unlawful for a governmental agency to deny anyone a right, benefit, or privilege merely because the individual refuses to disclose his or her SSN.

In Canada, each citizen has a social insurance number (SIN). The SIN is a nine-digit number created in 1964 to serve as a client account number in the administration of various Canadian government programs. It is a confidential number and its use is restricted to income-reporting purposes. There are a select and limited number of federal government departments and programs specifically authorized to collect the SIN. In addition, an employer can collect an employee's SIN to provide him or her with a record of employment and T4 slips for income tax purposes, as can provincial or municipal agencies to report financial assistance payments for income tax purposes. Institutions from which a Canadian citizen earns interest or income, such as banks, credit unions, and trust companies, can also collect the SIN.

The SSN or SIN is one of the numbers most prized by ID thieves. With it, they can apply for a number of other identity cards in your name. However, you can take steps to protect it:

- Never carry your SSN or SIN card, or any other card with that number printed on it.

- Never give your number to anyone by telephone, even if you make the call.

- Avoid having your SSN or SIN used for identification at work. Request a different number, if possible.

- Do not use your SSN or SIN as your driver's license number. Request that the Department of Motor Vehicles use an alternative number. Most states or provinces will provide one.

- Do not write your SSN or SIN on your checks, and do not have checks printed with it.

- Ensure that those requesting your SSN or SIN are doing so for legitimate rather than merely bureaucratic reasons.

The US Social Security Administration states on their website, www.ssa.gov, that "it is a very good idea to apply for a number right after your baby is born." If you decide to take that advice, guard that number as carefully as you do your own. There have been a number of cases of a child's SSN being stolen and used by ID thieves.

In the United States, request a copy of your Social Security Personal Earnings and Benefit Estimate Statement at least every three years to make certain the information in the file is correct. Contact the Social Security Administration at 1-800-772-1213 to learn how to order this free report.

A resident of Canada can request a copy of his or her official Canada Pension Plan Statement of Contributions once in any 12-month period. You can order this statement online at www.sdc.gc.ca/en/isp/cpp/soc/proceed.shtml.

If you reside in Quebec, you must contact www.rrq.gouv.qc.ca/en/.

CANADIAN FIREARMS LICENSE

In Canada, you must obtain a firearms license to purchase a weapon.

To get this license you must complete a firearms course and provide ID, but it would not be impossible for an identity thief to get a license using your stolen ID. A thief could also submit a change of address with the license number, last name, birth date, and place of birth.

If the thief purchased a weapon in this way, he or she could use it to commit a crime. As the weapon would be registered to you, it could cause you a great deal of trouble.

At this time, there are no public records of a thief going to this much trouble to get a gun. They can far more easily get one illegally on the street. Nonetheless, you should exercise the same vigilance regarding your Canadian Firearms license as you do any other piece of ID. Don't carry it with you. Keep it in a locked safe at home or in a safety deposit box.

IDENTITY THEFT INSURANCE

According to the American Insurance Information Institute, the fastest-growing insurance product is identity theft insurance. But is it really worth it?

Identity theft insurance doesn't fix your credit standing or clean up a criminal record acquired in your name by someone else. All it does is cover your expenses while you do this work yourself. On average, while attempting to clear himself or herself, an identity theft victim will ring up out-of-pocket costs of about $1,000, mainly for incidentals such as certified mail, notary seals, and phone calls.

The most highly advertised benefit is payment of lost wages for time taken from work. The Privacy Rights Clearinghouse in the United States estimates that victims on average spend the equivalent of 22 workdays cleaning things up. However, the common ID theft insurance maximum for lost wages is just $2,000.

The balance of the usual $5,000 to $15,000 coverage is available to pay for legal fees to undo judgments and clear criminal records racked up by thieves in your name. But Federal Trade Commission statistics show that just 16 percent of ID theft victims suffer such problems, and only 40 percent report out-of-pocket costs greater than $1,000.

Although identity theft insurance seems appealing, do not treat it as a safety net. You will still be liable for clearing your name and rebuilding your credit history.

"SAY NO" TO IDENTITY THEFT

To reduce the risk of becoming a victim of identity theft, teach your family the acronym SAY NO. When anyone asks for personal information, protect yourself by remembering the following:

S is for "Search"

Search all your credit and loan statements for any unfamiliar entries, large or small. Many identity thieves will charge a small amount — less than $5 — to a stolen card to see if it is noticed. If it isn't, they will proceed to max out the credit on the card.

If you do notice entries you don't recognize, react immediately. Contact the credit company and notify them that you could be a victim of identity theft and that you would like them to investigate these charges.

A is for "Ask"

Always ask anyone who wants your personal information why it is necessary for him or her to have it. For example, is the warranty on your purchase still valid if you do not fill in the warranty card and submit it? If you ever need to give up personal information, ask how it will be protected. If the person cannot give you a satisfactory answer, don't give away your data.

Y is for "You"

When purchasing goods or services either online or at a bricks-and-mortar location, remember that the seller is there to provide a service to you. You are the important part of the transaction, and *you* will decide if you will give them any personal information.

N is for "No"

It is okay to say no when someone asks for your information. There are very few organizations in this world that can legitimately demand your information. Companies are certainly not in that category.

O is for "Order"

Order a copy of your credit reports at least once a year. Your credit report will list all bank and financial accounts under your name and will tell you if someone has wrongfully opened or used any accounts in your name. You'll find instructions for requesting your annual credit report in Chapter 5.

Protect your information just as you do your family, and "Say No" to requests for information.

3

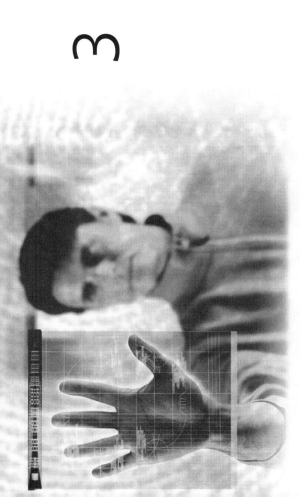

WHAT TO DO IF YOU BECOME A VICTIM

We have discussed how you can prevent yourself from becoming a victim of identity theft. Unfortunately, many people become victims even after they follow all the rules and have been very careful with their personal information.

For example, if a hacker stole your information from a company you trusted, like your bank or credit card company, there'd be little you could do to prevent it. But one day you'd get a call from a credit agency demanding money they believe you owe them. They might even threaten you with legal action. You'd realize that someone is using your identity to apply for credit and have to explain that you know nothing about the debt and you're a victim of identity theft.

It's likely that that first call would be followed by many from other creditors. You'd need to investigate how much damage had been done and set up a proper procedure to fix the array of problems you'd be facing.

Because identity theft is so personal, the steps you'd need to take would depend on your particular situation. However, the advice outlined in this chapter is designed to benefit anyone who finds himself or herself dealing with the consequences of this crime.

DOCUMENT EVERYTHING

Of course, in your effort to clear your name as well as your credit and possibly criminal records, you will have to contact numerous companies, agencies, and bureaus to let them know your identity has been stolen. But just as important as notifying such organizations of the theft is keeping paperwork on every action you take — including notes on whom you talked to, when, and what they said. If there is ever a disagreement with a creditor, these records could be invaluable. There is also the possibility that years after you have settled everything, your personal information could show up again in illegal transactions. Once your information is stolen, it is impossible to know when or if it will resurface. The records that you create now could be used as proof in the future to creditors that you've become a victim of identity theft once more.

So you need to set up a filing system to organize your paperwork — one that allows you quick access to it. A simple filing cabinet with labeled folders should work well.

Once you've cleared yourself with all concerned, be sure that you keep all the paperwork you generated and collected during the process. Not only can this be useful if your information resurfaces years later, but it also contains your personal data and must be guarded just like all your other valuable documents.

Before phoning a company with the news that your identity has been stolen, take some time to jot down all the issues you want to cover. For example, if someone acquired a credit card in your name, you'll want to get the exact date the application was made and find out if you can get a copy of the application.

As you discuss your situation, make notes to ensure you record everything. Write down all the information you receive during the call. Always make a note of the name and title of the person you spoke to, the department they work for, and any e-mail addresses or phone numbers you can use to contact them with follow-up questions. You could also record any follow-up action the company asks you to take and list any forms that the company asks you to submit. To ensure that you have understood everything the company's spokesperson says to you, paraphrase what you've heard the spokesperson say and then repeat it back to him or her.

If you don't feel you're getting the help you need, ask to speak to a supervisor.

TRACK YOUR INVESTIGATION

Accurate and complete records will greatly improve your chances of resolving your case. If you require legal assistance to settle some of your problems, your legal representative can use these records to help you win your case. The forms in Chapter 6 and on the enclosed CD will assist you in contacting the necessary organizations and keeping track of all the actions you take.

Complete a list of all contacts you have to make before you begin the process. (To get a quick start on this, use the Contacts Checklist you'll find in Chapter 6.)

As you work your way through your list, the procedures described below can help you accurately document your investigation:

- After you talk to a spokesperson, follow up the conversation with a letter to confirm in writing your understanding of what was said. This letter becomes part of your record of the conversation.

- When you do send mail as a follow-up, always request a return receipt and keep the receipt as part of your documentation. This is your proof that the company or agency received your correspondence.

- Note down any steps a company spokesperson asks you to take, including any documentation they request that you send them. Use your notes to ensure you take each step and send all the forms.

- If a company requires you to send in letters or forms, keep copies for your own records.

- Never send originals of necessary documents. Take a photocopy and send that, and keep the original for your own records.

- If you correspond by e-mail, keep a backup of all e-mails.

- Print all e-mails and keep a copy in your documentation.

- Record the names of all company or agency spokespersons you talk to, as well as the dates and times of the conversations.

- Record all the money you spent, including phone calls, postage, and time taken from work.

GET THE HELP YOU NEED

As you contact organizations to notify them of your problem, you'll find that most of the people you must deal with will be friendly and professional, as well as very helpful. They often know what you're going through and sympathize with you.

However, you will occasionally encounter people with little knowledge of how to handle identity theft. You will also encounter people who are simply uncooperative. This can be a frustrating and maddening experience.

Don't waste your time dealing with these employees. If they lack the knowledge to help you, yelling at them won't help. And if they're simply uncooperative, you don't have the time to talk them into doing their jobs.

If you find yourself in this situation, immediately ask to speak with a supervisor or another employee. If you meet with refusal, thank whomever you're talking to for his or her help and end the call. At a later date or time, call the organization again, and with a little luck, you'll reach someone else who can help you.

If you really cannot find anyone to assist you, do not give up. Send the company a registered letter explaining your situation. This will help protect your interests should you require reimbursement later.

WHOM YOU SHOULD CONTACT

What follows below is a simple summary of the companies, agencies, and government departments you must contact if you find that someone has stolen your identity. See Chapters 4 and 5 for detailed contact information, and Chapter 6 for forms to assist you.

Financial institutions

First, you must contact all the financial agencies that you deal with, including all your banks and credit card companies, to inform them that someone else has been making unauthorized financial transactions using your name.

You must make these calls immediately. The longer you wait, the more damage you could suffer. Don't assume that financial institutions will always cover your losses, no matter what. If you wait too long to inform them, they may not reimburse you. And be aware that some financial institutions may not cover any part of your losses if you did not protect your information.

Contact your branch and talk to the manager or supervisor. Ask if he or she has encountered identity theft before, and ask for an explanation of the steps you should take. If you are not happy with the responses, contact the head office. They may have a fraud department that can assist you.

If you know that your identity has been stolen, ask the financial institution to put a warning on your account. Also ask them to immediately close all your existing accounts and open new ones with new PINs and passwords. You should also shred any existing credit cards and debit cards immediately.

Many institutions will ask you to provide them with documentation, such as a police report. You can always send them the required paperwork later, but don't delay making the call.

You will also need to contact the credit reporting agencies. Credit reporting agencies are agencies that provide reports to lenders regarding your credit worthiness. (For example, if you apply for a car loan, the financing company will phone the credit bureaus to ask for your credit history.) Place a fraud alert with each of them, and they'll contact you each time they receive any requests for information — which means that if someone is applying for credit in your name, you'll know.

This verification process will not affect your credit rating, but it will stop identity thieves from making the situation worse. You should also order and review your credit reports. You'll find contact phone numbers and procedures for doing this in Chapter 5.

Police

You must file a police report, as most of the companies and agencies you'll be contacting will want a copy of this report. When you contact the local police, they will make a report about the incident.

Bring as much documentation as possible about your situation to the police station. This will include financial statements such as credit card bills and bank statements, and any other information you can acquire. The more documentation you can bring, the more complete the police report will be. But be sure to give the police only copies of these documents unless they demand the originals. Keep the originals for your own records. As you acquire more records (for example, future credit card statements), you should return to the police station and give them copies.

It will be your responsibility to gather all the required proof that you were a victim of identity theft. Identity theft is a non-violent, commercial crime, and the police may not consider it a high priority for investigation, which is why you'll need to do most of the footwork yourself. It is unlikely the police will contact each of your creditors for you.

Ask the police to give you a copy of this report. Some police departments will give you a copy of the report itself; others may issue a letter outlining the incident. This procedure will vary from community to community according to local policy. At the very minimum, the police will give you a file number.

The police report can also assist you should your information resurface years later and you require proof that this happened before. In addition, a filed report can act as a "red flag" to the police if someone is committing crimes in your name.

Personal service providers

Next, you'll need to get in touch with all your service providers, such as your telephone company or Internet service provider, to ensure that no one has ordered services in your name. Again, time is important. The longer you wait to inform your service providers, the greater the damage that can be done.

Confirm with the post office that no one has issued a change of address in your name. Notify them if you suspect that your mail is being stolen.

Contact all your Internet service providers and change your account information and passwords.

If you were a victim of a phishing scheme, notify your Internet service provider. Perhaps they can prevent others from becoming victims.

Contact all department stores and companies with which you have accounts, even if these are not credit accounts. Someone may apply for a credit account in your name.

Contact any brokerage firms with which you've done business and inform them.

Contact all utility companies as well, such as your electricity and heating providers, your cable TV supplier, and your telephone company.

Government departments

There are also a number of government departments you'll need to inform of the theft of your identity.

Contact your local passport office to find out if a passport has been issued in your name. They will issue you a new passport and put a warning flag on the passport number that the thief has stolen. If the identity thief uses the passport at a border crossing or airport, the warning will appear.

Contact your local driver's license issuing office to ensure no driver's license was issued in your name. If one was, have them cancel the license and issue you a new one. They will put a warning on the driver's license number that was incorrectly issued in your name. This warning will show up if the police stop the identity thief for a driving offense, or if he or she is arrested and presents it as identification.

If your social security card or social insurance card is missing, immediately notify the appropriate government office. See Chapter 4 for instructions and contact information.

To prevent tax fraud, notify the tax department. Ask them to report all recent transactions regarding your income to ensure no one is working under your name and not paying the proper taxes. The tax department can also tell you if they issued a tax refund check in your name that you did not receive.

You must also check in with any other government department that may have issued any cards to you or with which you have had dealings. You may have a card issued from a government health insurance program, or have registered a gun with government authorities. Contact them and tell them about your situation. Follow any instructions they give you.

BE SURE TO FOLLOW UP

Clearing your name will be a long and sometimes arduous process. As already mentioned, you will have to record the names and numbers of everyone you talked to, but equally as important, you will have to follow up with each one of them in writing.

Some departments may place your case on the back burner if they are busy. It's up to you to confirm they did as they said they would. Keep a diary of all your contacts and note down the date on which you need to follow up with them. For example, if a government agency said they'd investigate and get back to you in three weeks, make an entry on a calendar to contact them again in the stated time and ask for a progress report. Following up on every contact you make will be entirely your responsibility.

Some of the representatives you speak with will be very efficient and very helpful. Some may need some prodding. You are the only person you can rely on to ensure nothing is missed.

SUMMARY

Resolving the theft of your identity can be both time-consuming and costly. However, by following the procedures in this book and using the accompanying forms, you can ensure that you've missed nothing. You owe it to yourself to be thorough.

Be persistent. Be demanding. Record everything. And be patient with yourself.

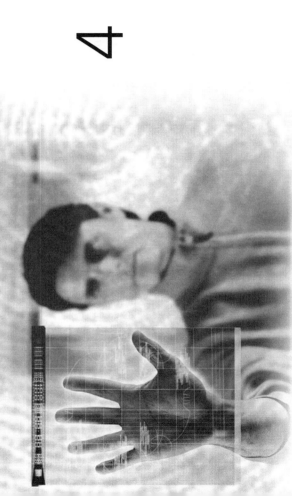

4

REPORTING AN IDENTITY THEFT

In this chapter, you'll find detailed contact information, including phone numbers and addresses, for the organizations you'll need to notify in the process of clearing your name, credit rating, and criminal records. If there are different contacts for the United States and for Canada, each is listed separately.

Remember, though, that some organizations have strict limits on the amount of time that can pass between you realizing your identity has been stolen and your reporting the situation to them. It's in your interests to act immediately.

LAW ENFORCEMENT

As soon as you realize that your identity has been stolen, inform your local police. Some financial agencies will require that you complete a police report before they reimburse you for your losses.

The contact information for your local police station can be located in the front of your community telephone book or in the section under municipal government. Do not call 911 to report identity theft, as that number is for emergencies only. You can complete the ID Theft Victim Information Form (see Chapter 6 or use the electronic copy on the enclosed CD) and give it to the police to aid them in completing their report.

Some police departments will provide you with a copy of the police report. However, others will only do so if you make the request in writing. In some cases they may only release the file number. In others, they may give you a letter stating they took a police report. Take what you can get.

For more information on filing a police report, see Chapter 3.

FINANCIAL REPORTING

To minimize your financial liability for any unauthorized transactions an identity thief may complete in your name, contact all financial institutions with which you do business, as well as any companies whose credit cards you hold, as soon as you suspect your personal information has been stolen.

After you contact them by phone, always follow up with a registered letter. For more information on financial reporting, see Chapter 3.

Financial institutions

You can usually find the contact numbers of your financial institutions — banks and credit unions — on any statements you've received from them. If you warn them of the theft as soon as possible after you discover it, they may be able to assist you in preventing further losses.

Credit card companies

After you've contacted your financial institutions, contact all your credit card companies. If your charge cards are from the same institution you bank with, the staff there may be able to assist you with both issues at the same time. There is usually a phone number on the back of the card. If your card has been stolen, check the photocopy you'll have made of it (see Chapter 2) or your credit card statements for the contact number.

Again, if you delay contacting these companies, they may not reimburse all your losses. Ensure that you replace all your credit cards with new ones, and confirm the address the company has on file for you. In many cases, the identity thieves have changed this information.

Debit cards

If you suspect someone has a debit card issued in your name, contact your financial institution immediately. Cancel the card and get a new one. Ensure you change your PIN and passwords.

Check cashing

Some identity thieves will open checking accounts in your name. Subsequently, you may receive notices of bounced checks from companies to which you have never written checks. There are a number of check-verification companies used by retail stores to verify your checks. If someone has opened a checking account in your name, contact these companies immediately to notify them. (See the list below for contact numbers.) These companies keep records on your check-cashing habits, and based on your history, will approve or decline the checks for the retailer.

Each of the check-verification companies has a telephone number you can use to report the theft of your identity. Unfortunately, at this time, there is no single number you can call to notify them all.

United States

TeleCheck: 1-800-710-9898
Global Payments Check Service: 1-866-860-9061
Certegy Inc.: 1-800-437-5120

Canada

TeleCheck: 1-800-366-2425
Certegy Inc.: 1-800-770-3792

Student loan fraud

United States

Contact the school or program that opened the student loan. If you've received requests for payment of a student loan you did not apply for, contact the school where the loan was opened. At the same time, report the fraudulent loan to the US Department of Education.

Call the Inspector General's Hotline toll free at 1-800-MIS-USED (1-800-647-8733).

You can also write to the department at —

Office of Inspector General
US Department of Education
400 Maryland Avenue SW
Washington, DC 20202-1510
Website: www.ed.gov/about/offices/list/oig/hotline
.html?src=rt

Canada

Student loans in Canada are handled both at the federal and provincial levels. The federal department that handles student loans is called Human Resources and Skills Development Canada (HRSDC).

They in turn use a company called the National Student Loans Service Centre (NSLSC) to handle the paperwork for the loans. If you want to find out if a loan has been issued in your name or under your SIN, you can contact them at the following website:

https://pub.canlearn.ca/CSLPIWeb/contactusStartPage.do

Alternatively, you can call them toll free at 1-888-815-4514. (Press "0" to talk to a representative.) Their offices are open Monday to Friday between 8:00 a.m. and 8:00 p.m., local time.

Explain to them you think you may be a victim of identity theft and want to confirm no student loans exist in your name.

Bankruptcy fraud

United States

Some ID thieves will try to file for bankruptcy in your name. Doing so allows them to avoid paying debts they've accumulated in your name and hide their own assets from the bankruptcy trustee.

For example, the identity thief may lease a residence and obtain credit under your name. When he or she accumulates a large debt load, he or she files for bankruptcy under your name to escape the consequences.

The US Trustee in your region can confirm if someone has filed for bankruptcy in your name. The United States Trustee Program is a part of the Department of Justice and assists law enforcement agencies like the FBI in the investigation of bankruptcy fraud.

A listing of the offices for the US Trustees can be found at www.usdoj.gov/ust/ under the link US Trustee Regions and Offices. Each region has its own website with details on whom you should call or e-mail.

Canada

In Canada, bankruptcy is handled by the Office of the Superintendent of Bankruptcy Canada.

This agency keeps a database of all bankruptcies filed in Canada since 1978. You can search online for your name for a fee of $8 at —

> https://strategis.ic.gc.ca/sc_mrksv/bankruptcy
> /bankruptcySearch/engdoc/

Department store accounts

Contact the store's credit department. The department store's general number can be found in the telephone book. Once you reach them, ask for the credit department. Cancel your cards and have the store place a fraud warning on your file.

Also check the address and contact information they have on file for you. Often an identity thief may give a change of address to the store so that you do not see your statements. If the store does have a new address on file, submit it to the local police so they can investigate it.

Investment fraud

You may receive a brokerage statement in the mail that you know nothing about. Or you may get a phone call from a broker trying to verify stock information on accounts you never opened. These are indications that someone may be using your identity to commit investment fraud.

United States

If you think someone may be trying to complete stock transactions or open an account in your name, report it to your broker or account manager immediately. Also contact the Securities and Exchange Commission (SEC). It is their mandate to protect consumers in the securities market. You can contact them through the website, address, or phone number listed below.

You can file a complaint with the SEC's Complaint Center —

www.sec.gov/complaint.shtml

You can also write to the SEC at —

SEC Office of Investor Education and Assistance
450 Fifth Street NW
Washington, DC 20549-0213

For answers to general questions, call (202) 942-7040.

Canada

If you think someone may be trying to complete stock transactions or open an account in your name, contact the branch manager of the brokerage firm immediately, as well as your local police force.

Also contact the Investment Dealers Association of Canada (IDA). Their website is www.ida.ca.

They also have branches in Montreal, Toronto, Calgary, Vancouver, and Halifax:

Montreal

Suite 2802
1 Place Ville Marie
Montreal, QC H3B 4R4
Tel: (514) 878-2854
Fax: (514) 878-3860
Enforcement matters only fax: (514) 878-6324

Toronto

Suite 1600
121 King Street West
Toronto, ON M5H 3T9
Tel: (416) 364-6133
Fax: (416) 364-0753
Enforcement matters only fax: (416) 364-2998

Calgary

Suite 2300
355 Fourth Avenue SW
Calgary, AB T2P 0J1
Tel: (403) 262-6393
Fax: (403) 265-4603
Enforcement matters only fax: (403) 234-0861

Vancouver

Suite 1325
PO Box 11614
650 West Georgia Street
Vancouver, BC V6B 4N9
Tel: (604) 683-6222
Fax: (604) 683-3491
Enforcement matters only fax: (604) 683-6262

Halifax

Suite 1620
TD Centre
1791 Barrington Street
Halifax, NS B3J 3K9
Tel: (902) 423-8800
Fax: (902) 423-0629

Investors wishing to inquire about making a complaint may call the IDA's toll-free line at 1-877-442-4322. The IDA will also mail you a copy of their customer complaint form, or you can find instructions and a copy to print at —

www.ida.ca/Investors/ResolveComplaint_en.asp#Filing

GOVERNMENT AGENCIES

There are a number of government agencies you will have to contact to ensure your personal information is correct.

Tax fraud

United States

If you suspect someone is committing tax fraud in your name, you must contact the IRS. You can make a report toll free to 1-800-829-0433, or you can write to them at the service center where you file your return. A listing of addresses can be found at —

www.irs.gov/file/index.html

After discussing your case with you, they may refer the matter to the IRS Criminal Investigation (CI) unit, which investigates any criminal violations. Information on this unit can be found at —

www.irs.gov/compliance/enforcement/article
/0,,id=98205,00.html

Canada

If you suspect someone is committing tax fraud in your name, you must contact the Canada Revenue Agency (CRA) either in person, by phone, or by regular mail. For security reasons, the CRA will not accept e-mails.

The CRA's website provides information on whom you should contact in your local area:

www.cra-arc.gc.ca/agency/investigations /province_tax-e.html

Driver's license
United States

If your driver's license has been lost or stolen, you should report it to the local police and your local Department of Motor Vehicles. The contact information for the police and the Department of Motor Vehicles is in your local phone book. However, the Department of Motor Vehicles does not take any legal action in these cases unless there is reason to suspect that your license is being used fraudulently.

Canada

In Canada, the reporting procedures for a stolen driver's license differ from province to province. However, most provinces will require you to contact your local driver services center. Contact information can be found in your local phone book. They will issue you a new driver's license and note the theft. You should also report it to the local police.

SSN or SIN fraud
United States

You may get a request from the IRS to pay taxes on income you've never received from employers you've never worked for. This could indicate someone is working under your SSN. In this case, you can contact the Social Security Administration to verify whether or not there is another taxpayer using your social security number.

The telephone number for the Social Security Administration is 1-800-772-1213.

They will request that you also contact the Federal Trade Commission (FTC) to file a complaint:

> Website: https://m.ftc.gov/pls/dod/widpubl$.startup?Z
> _ORG_CODE=PU03
> Tel: 1-877-ID-THEFT (1-877-438-4338)

Canada

If another person uses your social insurance number (SIN) to acquire employment or to receive other taxable income, you will receive a Notice of Reassessment from the Canada Revenue Agency concerning undeclared earnings. This is an indication that your SIN is being used fraudulently.

You can contact the CRA in person, by telephone, or by mail. They will not accept e-mails due to confidentiality rules. You can find a listing of all investigation units in Canada at —

> www.cra-arc.gc.ca/agency/investigations/province
> _tax-e.html

You should also contact your local Social Development Canada (SDC) office and notify them that your SIN is being used by someone else.

You will have to go to a local office to see an investigator. Addresses for each office in Canada can be found at —

> www.sdc.gc.ca/en/gateways/nav/top_nav/our
> _offices.shtml

You must complete the following steps before meeting an SDC investigator.

1. Go to your nearest Canada Revenue Agency Tax Services Office. Ask for a printout of all of the employers who issued a T4 slip for your SIN over the past three years. This printout, also known as a T4 Abstract, will list all the employers that have an employee whose SIN number matches yours. Ensure that this list includes all the employers' addresses.

2. Mark the names of any employers you have not worked for, but do not contact these employers. An SDC investigator

will contact them on your behalf. If you worked for all the names on the list and still think someone is using your SIN, contact your local SDC office for assistance.

3. Get one photograph of yourself for every employer you marked on the T4 Abstract. Photos from booths in malls or bus stations are acceptable.

4. Make a list of every address you have used for the last 10 years. Write down the dates you lived at each one.

5. Bring the list of employers, the photographs, the list of addresses and as many pieces of identification as you have to your local SDC office. They will require documented proof, such as a form indicating a reassessment of your income tax, and proof of identification, such as an original birth certificate.

You must also report the theft to the local police station and obtain a copy of the police report. The SDC will want a copy of the police report or a file number if the police will not release a copy.

The SDC will conduct a fraud investigation before issuing another number.

Passport fraud
United States

If you are a victim of identity theft, you should verify the thief has not taken out a passport in your name. Contact the United States Department of State (USDS). Their website is —

www.travel.state.gov/passport/passport_1738.html

They can also be reached by phone at the National Passport Information Center at 1-877-487-2778.

If your passport was lost or stolen, you should also report it to the US Department of State. The form for doing so is available on their website:

www.travel.state.gov/passport/forms/ds64/ds64 _845.html

The form states where to forward the completed document.

You can also call your local USDS field office. Local field offices are listed in the Blue Pages of your telephone directory.

Canada

If you suspect passport fraud, you are required to report it immediately to the local police and the local passport office. The address and phone number of your passport office and local police department can be found in the Blue Pages of your phone book.

If your passport is lost or stolen from you while you are away from home, report it to the local police and to the nearest Canadian embassy. The Canadian embassy phone number and location can be found in the local phone book of most cities. The local police or your hotel may also be able to give you the location.

Old Age Pension fraud
United States

In the US, there are a variety of different categories of pension plans. For example, there are employment-based retirement plans, multi-employer plans (for the union workforce), and individual retirement accounts. Within each category are a number of distinct types of plans.

This means that there is no single source that controls pension plans in the United States. However, you can contact the Social Security Administration to verify whether or not there is another taxpayer using your social security number.

The telephone number for the Social Security Administration is 1-800-772-1213. If you suspect tax fraud, contact the Internal Revenue Service (IRS) at 1-800-829-0433.

Canada

If you are a victim of identity theft, you should make certain no one is receiving OAS or CPP benefits in your name. You can view your records on the Government of Canada website at —

www.sdc.gc.ca/en/isp/common/proceed/vupipns.shtml

But before you can get this information from the website, you will need a personal access code. Apply for the code at —

www.sdc.gc.ca/en/isp/common/proceed/pacinfo.shtml

However, be aware that the code will be mailed to the address they have on file for you.

To use the online service, you must —

- live in Canada,

- receive payments under either OAS or CPP,

- provide your social insurance number, first name, last name, date of birth, and your mother's last name at her birth, and

- have a personal access code.

If you prefer to call them, or you have used the online service and found out there is a fraud, you can phone the following numbers:

For service in English: 1-800-277-9914
For service in French: 1-800-277-9915
TTY device: 1-800-255-4786

Agents are available Monday to Friday from 8:30 a.m. to 4:30 p.m. local time and from 9:00 a.m. to 5:00 p.m. in Newfoundland and Labrador. They will request your social insurance number.

You can also make an appointment to talk to a service agent in person. To locate an office near you, call the local Social Development Canada centre by looking in your local phone book under the government section, or go to their website at —

www.sdc.gc.ca/en/gateways/nav/top_nav/our
_offices.shtml

The Canadian government also has a website that provides information on replacing government-issued identification cards and what to do if you lose your wallet. In addition, it provides information on identity theft:

http://servicecanada.gc.ca/en/idcards/idcards.html

There is also a site devoted to ID theft at —

www.safecanada.ca/identitytheft_e.asp

CRIMINAL RECORDS

If your personal information has been stolen, you should always do a criminal records check. It is the only way to make certain that your identity has not been used by a criminal to avoid having to face charges himself or herself.

United States

There are two places you can check for criminal records in the United States:

Local police

You can request a criminal records search from your local police. The fees for this service vary from state to state. If you have moved from the area where you think your identification was stolen, contact the police in the area you lived when it occurred.

Once the police have concluded this search, they will give you a document stating the outcome of the check. If there are charges on your record that you know nothing about, the police will investigate. Each investigation will be conducted by that police department, and the length of and methods used in the investigation will vary. You will simply have to wait until they can prove there was a fraud and can correct the record.

Federal Bureau of Investigation

The Criminal Justice Information Services (CJIS) Division of the Federal Bureau of Investigation (FBI) centralizes justice information and provides information to local, state, federal, and international law enforcement, the private sector, and other government agencies. You can get instructions on how to request a criminal records check at —

www.fbi.gov/hq/cjisd/fprequest.htm

At that site, you'll find a copy of a cover letter that you must print and sign. The FBI will request original cards for proof of identity, fingerprints, and US $18 payable to the Treasury of the United States. It will take six to eight weeks to process your request. At that time, you will receive either a "No Record Response" or a "FBI Identification Record."

If there are charges against you and you wish to contest them, you will have to contact the submitting agency. For example, if the charges were submitted by your local police department, you must contact them. They will supply the guidelines for challenging the records. These guidelines will differ from state to state.

Canada

Under the Privacy Act of Canada, you can access your criminal records at any time from the RCMP or your local police. The RCMP's contact information is listed in your local telephone book in the Blue Pages at the back of the book. If there are no convictions on your record, they can provide you with a letter confirming that fact.

The RCMP or local police may request a copy of your fingerprints, and there could be a small charge associated with your request. The fingerprint charge is usually about $25, and the criminal check fee is about the same. (However, fees can vary slightly from province to province.)

If your criminal records are incorrect, you can request corrections from the RCMP or local police. You will have to visit your police station, and they will complete the proper forms, request photo identification, and take your fingerprints. There will also be a fee of approximately $50.

CANADIAN FIREARMS LICENSE

You could receive a notification from the Canadian Firearms Centre (www.cfc-ccaf.gc.ca) that a license has to be renewed for a firearm you do not own. Or perhaps you do own a firearm but its license is not due for renewal. Either of these events could indicate that someone took out a firearms license in your name.

Immediately phone the Canada Firearms Centre at 1-800-731-4000 to notify them and request that they search their records for any information on how this license came to be issued or why the renewal has come up ahead of time.

However, the Canada Firearms Centre will also ask you to submit your request through the Coordinator, Office of Access to Information and Privacy, even in the case of fraud. You can contact them at —

Coordinator, Office of Access to Information and Privacy
Canada Firearms Centre
10th Floor
50 O'Connor Street
Ottawa, ON K1A 1M6

For advice on how to make this request, you can phone 1-800-731-4000, extension 2055.

You can find the Request for Information Form at —

www.tbs-sct.gc.ca/tbsf-fsct/350-57_e.asp

PERSONAL REPORTING

As mentioned in Chapter 3, an identity thief may order services in your name. If the thief gives the service provider a billing address other than your home, it may be months before you realize what's happened. Your first indication could be calls from a debt collection agency, or you may apply for credit and be surprised to find it denied because of a bad credit rating.

If any of your personal information is stolen, or if you've had any indication that someone may be using your identity for any purpose, notify all your service providers immediately.

Phone fraud

United States

If you discover that a thief has used your identity to obtain phone service, get in touch with the phone company right away. Tell them about your situation and ask them to close the account.

If the telephone company disputes your claim, you may be able to get help from the Public Utility Commission if the service was local or from the Federal Communications Commission (FCC) if the fraud involved cellular phones or long distance service. Each state has its own Public Utility Commission, and the contact information can be found in your local phone book. You can call the FCC at —

1-888-CALL-FCC (1-888-225-5322)
TTY: 1-888-TELL-FCC (1-888-835-5322)

Or you can write to the FCC at —

Federal Communications Commission
Consumer Information Bureau
Room 5A863
445 12th Street SW
Washington, DC 20554

You can also file complaints online at www.fcc.gov, or e-mail your questions to fccinfo@fcc.gov.

Canada

If an identity thief has established phone service in your name, contact the telephone company and have it canceled immediately. You can usually find the company's phone number on your bill. Also check your current statements on your existing account to ensure all the records are accurate. If there are calls that you do not recognize, close the account and open a new one.

If your phone provider is not assisting you in investigating incorrect charges or accounts, you can contact the Canadian Radio-Television and Telecommunications Commission (CRTC). Their website is —

www.crtc.gc.ca

Click the "Complaints and Inquiries" link in the menu on the left of the page.

You can also phone them toll free at —

1-877-249-2782
TDD line: 1-877-909-2782

Or contact them by mail at —

CRTC
Ottawa, ON K1A 0N2

(No PO Box or street address is necessary)

Calling cards

Report the loss or theft of your calling cards to the appropriate long distance company as soon as possible to minimize the risk of abuse by thieves.

Utility fraud

If someone has established utilities such as electricity or heating in your name, immediately contact your local providers. Their contact information is in your local phone book.

Mail theft

United States

Contact your local office of the Postal Inspection Service if you suspect that an identity thief has submitted a change-of-address form with the post office to redirect your mail or has used your mail to commit fraud involving your identity. The address and contact information listed are under the government section of your local phone book. You should also notify your local police department.

Canada

Your local Canada Post office is capable of taking any reports on mail theft. However, as mail theft is a serious crime, they may also ask you to report the incident to the police.

Internet fraud

If you attempt to log in to your Internet service and find that you cannot, it's possible that your password has been changed by someone else. Immediately contact your Internet service provider (ISP). They will restore your service and follow up on who made the change. Also verify your current address and billing information with them to ensure your bills are not being sent to the wrong address.

If you receive unauthorized service bills from an ISP, it could mean someone has established service in your name. You should contact that service provider immediately. Their phone number should be shown on the bill. Or, if you go to their website, you'll find a "Contact Us" button on their menu. If you select it, you'll find the phone numbers or mailing address of the ISP. They will assist you in closing the account.

If you suspect a thief has applied for or established an account in your name with companies such as eBay or Amazon, contact the company immediately. Every company website is different; however, you can usually find a "Contact Us" button in the menu on their home page. Select it, and you'll find numbers for customer service. Call and inform them that you do not have an account with them and someone else is using your identity. They will tell you what you need to do to close the account.

You should also do a web search on your name. It's possible that you could find your personal information on websites you know nothing about. For example, in one case, an individual compiled a family tree and posted it on his website. The tree showed the entire names, birth dates, and addresses of each of his family members. The release of even that much information could lead to identity theft.

You also want to ensure employers do not post your full name, job description, and telephone number on their websites. Personal data should not be released to the public.

Whatever search engine you use, perform a search on your full name surrounded by double quotes (for example, "Bill Victim"). Enter a few different variations of your name (use your middle name or initials) to make the search as thorough as possible.

No one search engine will find everything you are looking for, so use several.

If you do find your personal data on a website, you should contact the owner of the site and request they immediately remove it. If they refuse, you may need to seek legal counsel.

HELP TRACK IDENTITY THEFT

The governments of both Canada and the US are compiling statistics on identity theft and asking for public cooperation in this task. These statistics can help the appropriate agencies learn new methods of fighting this crime.

If you are a victim of identity theft, report it to one of the following agencies. They cannot assist you in clearing your name, but by reporting your experience to them, you can help others affected by identity theft. Be a crime reporter.

United States Federal Trade Commission

In the United States, the Federal Trade Commission (FTC) is the central location to report identity theft. They have an Identity Theft Reporting Hotline at 1-877-ID-THEFT (1-877-438-4338), where counselors will take your complaint. However, they will not contact any creditors, law enforcement agencies, or service providers on your behalf. (You must do that yourself.)

The FTC will advise you to place a fraud warning with the credit bureaus in the United States and to file a police report. The FTC is using the compiled statistics you provide to help stop identity theft.

PhoneBusters Canada

PhoneBusters is a central sourcing location for pertinent information on identity theft and phone scams in Canada. They track current trends and patterns and use the information to assist law enforcement agencies with possible investigations. However, they cannot assist you in repairing your credit or clearing your name. You must do that yourself. Contacting PhoneBusters is optional.

Tel: 1-888-495-8501
E-mail: info@phonebusters.com
Website: www.phonebusters.com

5

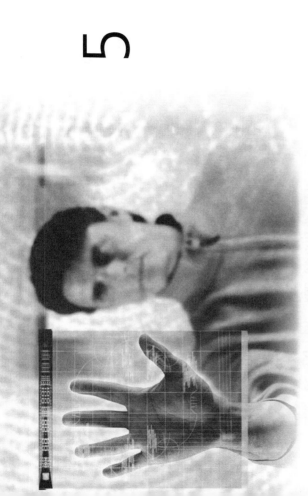

YOUR CREDIT REPORT

You may not be aware of it, but each time you apply for credit with any financial organization or company, a record of that application is stored with a credit reporting agency. Each time you pay a bill late, the company involved reports the late payment to a credit reporting agency. Credit reporting agencies (also called credit bureaus) are constantly gathering information on your credit worthiness. They also keep a record of your personal information, such as your employment history and current and past addresses.

Whenever you apply to a financial institution for a loan, apply to a credit company for a card, apply to rent a dwelling from a landlord, or, under some circumstances, apply to a potential employer for a new job, the people to whom you are making the application contact the credit reporting agencies and request your file to discover how creditworthy you are. If there are negative entries in your file, such as records stating you haven't made a bill payment for 90 days, or have ever defaulted on a loan, or that you've made too many applications for credit during a given period, you could be turned down on loans or rejected as a potential tenant or employee.

Credit reporting agencies started as local associations of merchants, and credit reports were given by word of mouth. Now they are much more regulated and follow strict reporting guidelines.

Credit reporting agencies get their information from three major sources:

1. Consumers themselves, who supply information, primarily on applications for credit.

2. Public records, which provide information on bankruptcies, foreclosures, court judgments, and agreements registered with provincial authorities.

3. Credit grantors and collection agencies, which send their files electronically to the credit reporting agencies every month. (These files include the account number, the outstanding balance, and a nine-point scale indicating whether a payment was made on time or late.)

Your credit report could include —

- your name, addresses, date of birth, and employer's details;

- a history of payments with credit grantors such as retail stores, banks, finance companies, and mortgage companies;

- items that may affect your creditworthiness, such as judgments, bankruptcies, and registered items;

- a list of credit grantors and other parties you have authorized to receive your credit information; and

- information that could include banking information and collections.

You have the right to examine your file and to explain or correct any information. In fact, it's in your best interest to do so, as credit reports can be a very important tool in detecting identity theft. Check your credit reports at least once a year to see if there are any entries you do not recognize, since this could be an indication that someone's been using your personal information. For example, if you see credit applications from a bank or a company, and you have never made these applications, they could be signals that you've become a victim of identity theft.

If you suspect that your identity has been stolen, you can place a fraud alert with the credit reporting agencies, which will help to prevent any further credit damage. If someone attempts to get credit using your name and your report shows a fraud alert, it is unlikely the credit will be approved.

Having a credit alert on your file does not damage your credit. It simply means that when a company receives an application for credit in your name, it will contact you personally to confirm that you — not a thief — have made the application.

CREDIT REPORT SUSPICIONS

When you get your credit report, examine it closely for any entries you don't recognize. Any of the following may signal a problem:

- Any credit inquiries from companies to which you never applied for credit
- Name changes
- Address changes
- Employment changes
- New accounts
- Closed accounts
- Strange account balances
- Credit limit changes
- Collection accounts
- Bankruptcy filings
- Tax liens
- Judgments
- International credit card applications

If you see any entries that seem puzzling, investigate them right away. Let's say you see an application inquiry from a credit card company, but you know you never applied to them for a card. Contact that company immediately. Tell them that you've just reviewed your credit report and seen an inquiry from them on it, but that you did not fill out any application for a card with them. Ask them why that entry has appeared, and get as much information from them as possible.

If, in fact, someone else *is* making credit applications in your name, immediately place a fraud alert with the credit reporting agencies.

As the credit reporting systems differ slightly between Canada and the United States, the rest of this chapter is divided into a discussion of the two systems.

UNITED STATES CREDIT BUREAUS

There are three national credit bureaus in the United States: TransUnion, Equifax, and Experian.

None of the three national credit bureaus shares information with the others. Therefore, you will have to check with all three credit bureaus to get a complete picture of the true state of your credit report. Please note that each of the three major credit reporting agencies offers a service that will sell you a credit report from all three agencies for a single fee. This means you will not have to go through the process of acquiring one from each agency.

There are also dozens of smaller credit bureaus throughout the United States. They are sometimes referred to as consumer reporting agencies and serve specialized markets. However, most credit grantors who report to them will also report to at least one of the three major agencies listed above. Therefore, you need only contact the major three and not the smaller ones.

Fraud alert

If you are a victim of identity theft, you must contact each of the national credit reporting agencies to place a fraud alert on your files. These fraud alerts are free of charge.

The fraud alert will remain on file for up to seven years. If at any time you wish to have the alert removed, you can submit a written request. As mentioned above, a fraud alert does not damage your credit rating; however, companies to which you've applied for credit will contact you personally to verify your identity.

Forms and sample letters to assist you in dealing with the credit reporting agencies are available in Chapter 6.

Your rights

The Fair Credit Reporting Act (FCRA) is an American federal law that regulates how consumer credit information is collected and used by credit reporting agencies. It also regulates the responsibilities of these credit agencies, including the necessity of providing a consumer with copies of the information in their files, maintaining the accuracy of those files, and informing consumers about the steps the agencies take to protect those files.

Under this law, companies that provide consumer information have the obligation to verify any data the consumer feels is incorrect. The complete text of the Fair Credit Reporting Act can be found at www.ftc.gov/os/statutes/fcra.htm.

Here is a brief summary of some of the rights granted under the act:

- Any company that refuses you credit because of information they've received from a credit reporting agency must inform you and give you the name, address, and phone number of that agency.

- If you dispute information the credit reporting agency has in your file, that agency must investigate that information. The credit reporting agency must present the disputed information to the company that reported them, and if the data was incorrect, the credit reporting agency must give you a written report on the outcome.

- The credit reporting agency must give you a copy of the information in your file, including the names of everyone who recently requested a copy of your file.

- The credit reporting agency must remove any proven inaccurate information from your file.

- Any information older than seven years cannot be reported.

- Any bankruptcy information older than 10 years cannot be reported.

- The credit reporting agency must obtain written permission from you before giving any data to an employer.

- The credit reporting agency cannot give out any medical information without your written permission.

- If these rules are violated by a credit reporting agency, you can sue them in a state or federal court.

Under state law, you may have additional rights. These rights vary from state to state. To find out the laws for your state, contact the attorney general for your state or a local consumer protection agency.

The following agencies enforce the Fair Credit Reporting Act in their respective industries. Contact the appropriate agency if you have a complaint or concern.

Credit reporting agencies and creditors

Federal Trade Commission
Consumer Response Center — FCRA
Washington, DC 20580
Tel: (202) 326-3761

Federal branches of foreign banks and national banks

Office of the Comptroller of the Currency
Compliance Management, Mail Stop 6-6
Washington, DC 20219
Tel: 1-800-613-6743

Federal Reserve System member banks

Federal Reserve Board
Division of Consumer & Community Affairs

Washington, DC 20551
Tel: (202) 452-3693

Savings associations and federally chartered savings banks

Office of Thrift Supervision
Consumer Programs
Washington, DC 20552
Tel: 1-800-842-6929

Federal credit unions

National Credit Union Administration
1775 Duke Street
Alexandria, VA 22314
Tel: (703) 518-6360

State-chartered banks (not members of the Federal Reserve System)

Federal Deposit Insurance Corporation
Consumer Response Center
2345 Grand Avenue, Suite 100
Kansas City, MO 64108-2638
Tel: 1-800-378-9581

Free credit reports

There is normally a small fee you need to pay to obtain your credit report, but the FCRA states that you are entitled to a free personal credit report once every 12 months under the following circumstances:

- You were denied a loan or other credit because of information in the credit report. (You are entitled to a free credit report only from the reporting agency that supplied that information.)

- You are unemployed and intend to apply for a job within the next 60 days.

- You are receiving public assistance.

- You feel there are errors in your credit report resulting from fraud.

- You live in Colorado, Maryland, Massachusetts, New Jersey, or Vermont. (The state laws entitle you to one free credit report per year.)

- You live in Georgia. (State laws entitle you to two free reports per year.)

Free active duty alerts for military personnel

Active members of the military are sometimes posted to locations outside the country and are not able to monitor their credit information. Therefore, they could be more susceptible to fraud.

If you are an active member of the military, you can place an "Active Duty Alert" on your file at the credit bureaus for free. These alerts are kept on the file for 12 months, but can be extended if necessary.

If you place an Active Duty Alert on your files, any company that receives an application for credit from you must contact you directly by phone or other means to verify it really was you — not an identity thief — who placed that application. It also means you can get a free credit report once a year.

Credit report fees

Table 3 shows the current rates for a personal credit report.

If you don't qualify for a free personal credit report under the federal law, you may still be eligible for a reduced-price personal credit report based on state law.

Note: Each credit reporting agency allows you the option of purchasing a credit report from all three agencies at once. Doing so can save you the trouble of having to contact all three agencies and buying a report from each one.

Each company will also, for a fee, provide you with your credit score. A credit score is a numerical rating of your credit. The higher the number, the better your credit. The credit score is useful; however, it does not assist you in discovering if an identity thief is applying for credit in your name. To verify your credit entries, you must get your credit report and check it thoroughly.

TransUnion

TransUnion is one of the three major credit reporting agencies in the United States. You can get a personal credit report from TransUnion; however, you must also check reports from the other two bureaus to ensure you have all the information available on your credit situation.

Table 3
Current Rates for a Personal Credit Report

State	1st request	2nd request	Additional	Time frame
California	$8.00	$8.00	$8.00	Any time
Colorado	Free	$8.00	$8.00	Calendar year
Connecticut	$5.00	$7.50	$7.50	12 months
Georgia	Free	Free	$9.00	Calendar year
Maine	Free	$5.00	$5.00	12 months
Maryland	Free	$5.00	$5.00	12 months
Massachusetts	Free	$8.00	$8.00	Calendar year
Minnesota	$3.00	$9.00	$9.00	12 months
Montana	$8.50	$8.50	$8.50	Any time
New Jersey	Free	$8.00	$8.00	12 months
Vermont	Free	$7.50	$7.50	12 months
US Virgin Islands	$1.00	$1.00	$1.00	Any time
All other states	$9.50	$9.50	$9.50	Any time

Credit file request

If you suspect that someone has stolen your identity, or want to check to make certain you are not a victim, request a copy of your credit file from TransUnion by any one of the following three methods:

Online

You can request an online copy of your credit report from Trans-Union's website. After you provide the required information to identify yourself and you supply a credit card number, your report will appear in your web browser so that you can print it out.

To get a copy of your credit report online —

1. log on to www.transunion.com,

2. click the "Personal Solutions" link on the menu at the top of the page,

3. click the "Order Now" button for the option you are requesting, and

4. complete the information screens, and click "Submit."

Mail

If you wish to receive a report by mail, you can complete the online request form you'll find at http://annualcreditreport.transunion .com/pdf/DisclosureRequest.pdf. The fee for this service will vary from state to state; the fee listing is on the form. You will need to include a check or money order payable to TransUnion for the applicable fee.

When you order by mail, TransUnion requires you to provide the following information:

- First, middle, and last name (including Jr., Sr., III)
- Current address
- Previous addresses in the past two years, if any
- Social security number
- Date of birth

- Current employer
- Phone number
- Signature

Ensure you sign and date the form before sending it.

Once you have completed the request form, mail it to —

TransUnion LLC
PO Box 1000
Chester, PA 19022

Also be aware that you can only obtain a credit report on yourself. If more than one member of your household is requesting a file, each individual must supply a separate request.

Phone

You can also request a credit report by phone by calling 1-800-888-4213.

You'll reach an automated system that takes your information. When you complete the call, your report will be mailed to you. The fee for this service will vary from state to state. You will be informed of the charges during the phone call.

Note: Obtaining a credit report under false pretenses is a federal crime.

The following pages contain a sample of a credit report from the TransUnion website.

Filing a fraud alert with TransUnion

If you suspect you are a victim of identity theft, you must place a fraud alert with all the major national credit bureaus. There is no fee for placing a fraud alerts.

To contact TransUnion's fraud department, phone 1-800-680-7289. You'll reach an automated phone system that allows you to add the alert. Once you have completed the call, a statement will be added to your file that asks any new creditors viewing your file to contact you personally before approving the application. This statement will remain on your file for one year.

SAMPLE CREDIT REPORT FROM TRANSUNION (US)

Note: This report example is only an illustration of the type of information provided when your TransUnion Personal Credit Report is ordered. The information in the report example does not reflect your personal situation. You must order your TransUnion Personal Credit Report to obtain the credit information that pertains to your personal situation.

Personal Information

Name: EXAMPLE TEST USER

You have been on our files since 05/1999

SSN: XXX-XX-0001

File Number: 123466789
Date Issued: Nov 16, 2004

Telephone (555) 555-1234x12345

Your SSN is partially masked for your protection

CURRENT ADDRESS

Address: 1100 CURRENT ST.
PERCITY, CA 10000

Reported: 09/2002

EMPLOYMENT DATA REPORTED

Employer Name: EMPLOYER 1
Date Reported: 06/2004

Position: JOB/OCCUPATION 1
Hired: 06/2004

Special Notes: Your Social Security number has been masked for your protection. You may be required to explain public record items to potential creditors. Any address found at the end of this report. Also, any item on your credit report that begins with 'MEDI' indicates medical information. The data following this word is not displayed to anyone but you, except where permitted by law.

Public Records

The following items obtained from public records appear on your report. You may be required to explain public record items to potential creditors. Any bankruptcy information will remain on your report for 10 years from the date of the filing. Unpaid tax liens may generally be reported for an indefinite period of time depending on your state of residence. Paid tax liens may be reported for 7 years from date of payment. All other public record information, including discharged chapter 13 bankruptcy and any accounts containing adverse information, remain for up to 7 years.

CRCITY MUNICIPAL   Docket#: 95C00558

Type:	Civil Judgment	**Date Filed:**	12/2002
Court Type:	Municipal	**Responsibility:**	Participant on account
Date Paid:	07/2004	**Plaintiff:**	BANK OF NEW YORK
Assets:	$1,079	**Plaintiff Attorney:**	PERRY MASON
		Amount:	$1,079

Estimated date that this item will be removed: 06/2009

Key to reading your payment history data.

Some creditors report how you make payments each month in relation to your agreement with them. The key below outlines how to read the payment history section for each account.

OK	30	60	90	120	
NA	Unknown	Current	30 days late	60 days late	90 days late	120 days late

Adverse Accounts

The following accounts contain information which some creditors may consider to be adverse. Adverse account information may generally be reported for 7 years from the date of the first delinquency, depending on your state of residence. The adverse information in these accounts has been printed in >brackets< or is shaded for your convenience, to help you understand your report. They are not bracketed or shaded this way for creditors. (Note: The account # may be scrambled by the creditor for your protection).

R DEPARTMENT ONE #000000000000000001

4401 E. CREDITOR S ST SUITE401
CRCITY, CA 40001
(800) 555-4000

Balance:	$153
Updated:	07/2004
High Balance:	$532
Opened:	01/1999
Past Due:	$0

Pay Status:	Paid or Paying as Agreed
Account Type:	Revolving account
Responsibility:	Individual account
Credit Limit:	$5,000
Loan Type:	Appliance/Furniture

Late Payments
(last 48 months)

| OK | 30 | 60 | 90 |
| 2 | 0 | 0 | 0 |

Last 4 Years

aug jul jun may apr mar feb '02 dec nov oct sep aug jul
aug jul jun may apr mar feb '01 dec nov oct sep aug jul
aug jul jun may apr mar feb '00 dec nov oct sep aug jul
aug jul jun may apr mar feb '99 dec nov oct sep

Satisfactory Accounts

The following accounts are reported with no adverse information.

OTHER FINANCE ONE #000000002

4402 E. CREDITOR S ST SUITE402
CRCITY, CA 40002
(800) 555-4001

Balance:	$0
Updated:	07/2004
High Balance:	$20,000
Opened:	05/1999
Past Due:	$0

Pay Status:	Paid or Paying as Agreed
Account Type:	Installment account
Responsibility:	Individual account
Credit Limit:	$0

Late Payments
(last 61 months)

| OK | 30 | 60 | 90 |
| 0 | 0 | 0 | 0 |

Last 4 Years

jun may apr mar feb '04 dec nov oct sep aug jul
jun may apr mar feb '03 dec nov oct sep aug jul
jun may apr mar feb '02 dec nov oct sep aug jul
jun may apr mar feb '01 dec nov oct sep aug jul

CREDIT CARD CO #000000003

1111 N. FAKESTREET WY
CRCITY, CA 40002
(800) 555-4002

Balance:	$0
Updated:	07/2004
High Balance:	$4,000
Opened:	03/2000
Past Due:	$0

Pay Status:	Paid or Paying as Agreed
Account Type:	Revolving account
Responsibility:	Individual account
Credit Limit:	$6,000

Late Payments
(last 51 months)

| OK | 30 | 60 | 90 |
| 0 | 0 | 0 | 0 |

Last 4 Years

jun may apr mar feb '04 dec nov oct sep aug jul
jun may apr mar feb '03 dec nov oct sep aug jul
jun may apr mar feb '02 dec nov oct sep aug jul
jun may apr mar feb '01 dec nov oct sep aug jul

Regular Inquiries

The following companies have received your credit report. Their inquiries remain on your credit report for two years.

INQUIRY ANALYSIS NAME 1
5501 NW. INQUIRY E ST., #501
INCITY, CA 50001

| Requested on: | 10/2004 |
| Inquiry Type: | Individual account |

Permissible Purpose: Employment

EXAMPLE INQUIRY COMPANY
1234 S. CREDIT ST., #123
ANYTOWN, IL 12345

| Requested on: | 06/2004 |
| Inquiry Type: | Individual account |

Permissible Purpose: Credit Transaction

Inquiry Analysis

The companies that request your credit report must first provide certain information about you. Within the past 90 days, companies that requested your report provided the following information.

INQUIRY ANALYSIS NAME 1

Requested on:	Identifying Information They Provided:
10/2004	EXAMPLE TEST USER
	1100 CURRENT ST.
	PERCITY, CA 10001

Promotional Inquiries

The companies listed below received your name, address and other limited information about you so they could make a firm offer of credit or insurance. They did not receive your full credit report, and these inquiries are not seen by anyone but you.

SAMPLE BANK
5678 MAIN RD.
SUITE 123
SOME CITY, VA 98765
(800)555-5555

Requested on: 03/06/2003

Account Review Inquiries

The companies listed below obtained information from your consumer report for the purpose of an account review or other business transaction with you. These inquiries are not displayed to anyone but you and will not affect any creditor's decision or any score (except insurance companies may have access to other insurance company inquiries, where permitted by law).

OTHER FINANCE ONE
4402 E. CREDITOR ST
CRCITY, CA 40002
(800) 555-4001

Requested on: 11/01/2002
Inquiry Type: Individual

SAMPLE INSURANCE CO
1111 N. FAKESTREET WY
CRCITY, CA 40002
(800) 555-4002

Requested on: 05/01/2004
Inquiry Type: Individual
Permissible Purpose: Insurance Underwriting

Consumer Statement

My wallet was stolen on June 19, 2004. Please ask for identification when you receive an application for credit.
(Note: This statement is set to expire in 12/2004.)

Special Messages

SECURITY ALERT: #HK#CACRA Consumer's identity may have been used without his or her consent. Recipients of this report are advised to verify the consumer's identity prior to issuing credit. Verify at 805 555-1212.
(Note: This statement is set to expire in 12/2004.)

Note: This report example is only an illustration of the type of information provided when your TransUnion Personal Credit Report is ordered. The information in the report example does not reflect your personal situation. You must order your TransUnion Personal Credit Report to obtain the credit information that pertains to your personal situation.

94 Identity theft toolkit

If at any time you wish to have the statement removed, or to extend it for more than one year, you can submit a written request. The letter need only state that you wish to extend or remove the alert. You must include proof of your address and phone number. An acceptable form of verification for your telephone number is a copy of your current phone bill. An acceptable form of verification for your address is a copy of one of the following items that displays your current address:

- Driver's license
- Utility bill
- Signed lease
- Bank or credit union statement
- Canceled check
- Signed homeless-shelter letter
- Medicaid or Medicare card
- Paycheck stub
- Stamped post office box receipt
- Prison ID
- State ID card
- W2 form

The mailing address of TransUnion's Fraud Victim Assistance Department is —

TransUnion
Fraud Victim Assistance Department
PO Box 6790
Fullerton, CA 92834

If you have general questions about being a victim of fraud, you can also e-mail TransUnion at fvad@transunion.com. However, if you e-mail them, do not include any personal information.

The FVAD Seven-Step Program

TransUnion's Fraud Victim Assistance Department (FVAD) has started a seven-step program to assist you in preventing and controlling the damage done by identity theft and to help you restore your credit file to its correct state.

The following description of the seven steps the FVAD takes is reprinted here with TransUnion's permission:

Step 1
Add a consumer fraud alert and remove the victim from mailing lists.

The FVAD will add a fraud alert to your credit file, advising any potential creditors to contact you before approving credit applications. This statement is retained on your credit file for seven years from the date it was added, or until you request its deletion in writing. Additionally, your name and address will not be included on any TransUnion mailing lists for two years.

Step 2
Highlight recent inquiries and/or accounts suspected as fraud.

After an FVAD representative verifies your identity, the representative advises you of any recent inquiries and/or accounts that are new to your file. If you are unaware of the inquiry and/or account, the phone representative provides the address and phone number for each. Moreover, the representative reminds you to notify the respective creditor of any fraudulent inquiry and/or account.

Step 3
Mail the credit file to the consumer.

After the phone call, an FVAD representative mails you a copy of your TransUnion credit file. Proof of identity and/or residency may be required to safeguard your file from further fraudulent activity.

Step 4

Mail educational material.

When the FVAD mails a credit file, we include a dispute form and educational material advising you of your responsibilities. We may also include tips on preventing future fraud. The material provided is based on the specific type of past or potential fraud.

Step 5

Notify joint-victim credit grantors.

Based on our conversation with you, the FVAD notifies credit grantors through fax or mail of a suspected fraud inquiry and/or account. Specifically, the FVAD advises the credit grantors to check for a recent application or opened account with the victim's identifying information. By approaching the fraud from both the consumer's and credit grantor's perspectives, a significant amount of fraud can be prevented.

Step 6

Keep a database of fraud information.

The FVAD adds fraud addresses, telephone numbers, and Social Security numbers to an internal database containing fraud information. Should this information be used on future fraudulent applications, an alert is generated advising potential credit grantors to check for fraud.

Step 7

Restore the victim's credit file to its accurate state.

The FVAD investigates any disputed credit information to restore your credit file to its accurate state.

Equifax

Equifax is another of the three major credit reporting agencies in the United States. You must check your Equifax report as well as your reports from the two other agencies.

Credit report request

You can request a copy of your credit report by any one of the following three methods:

Online

An online copy of your credit report can be requested from Equifax's website for a fee of $9.50. This report will appear in your web browser so you can print it out. Note that Equifax will also provide you with credit reports from all three major credit reporting agencies for $29.95.

To order a copy of your credit report from Equifax —

1. log on to www.equifax.com,

2. on the top menu, click "Products,"

3. click "Equifax Credit Report,"

4. click the "Order Now" button, and

5. complete the extensive request form and submit it.

Your credit report will appear in your browser in a printable format.

Mail or fax

You can request a copy of your credit report by mail. However, you cannot order only your credit report; you must order a product called Score Power for $14.94. This report includes your credit score as well as your credit report.

To order a copy of your credit score and credit report by mail or fax —

1. log on to www.equifax.com,

2. on the top menu, click "Products,"

3. click "Score Power,"

4. in the middle of the page, click the link that says "Or click here to fax your order,"

5. print out the form, and

6. complete, sign, and date it.

You can either fax the form or mail it. The fax number and address are shown at the bottom of the form. They will mail your information to you.

Phone

If you wish to get a credit report by phone, call Equifax at 1-800-685-1111, and a representative will assist you.

Filing a fraud alert with Equifax

You can place a fraud alert on your file by calling 1-888-766-0008. This number takes you to an automated phone system that places an immediate fraud alert on your file. Subsequently, a package will be mailed to you containing information on getting free credit reports and other helpful tips on identity theft and fraud. Once Equifax processes your fraud alert, they will notify the other two credit reporting agencies, and each of them will also place fraud alerts in your files.

If you prefer, you may write to the Equifax's Consumer Fraud Division at the following address:

Equifax
Consumer Fraud Division
PO Box 740256
Atlanta, GA 30374

Equifax asks that you include your name, address, social security number, date of birth, and telephone number(s) in your letter. If you do not wish to send all this information by mail, you could request them to contact you by phone upon receipt of your letter. Inform them that you are a victim of identity theft and wish a fraud alert placed on your file.

Experian

Experian is the third major credit bureau agency in the United States. You must ensure that you check your Experian credit report as well as those from the other two bureaus.

Credit file request

You can request a copy of your credit report from Experian by the following methods:

Online

You can request an online copy of your credit report for a fee of $9.50. To do this —

1. log on to Experian's website at www.experian.com,

2. click the drop-down menu at the top right of the page and select "United States,"

3. find the link that says "Experian credit report" and click the "Order now" button, and

4. complete each page of the form and submit it.

Your report will open in a web browser you can print.

Mail

You can request a credit report be sent to you by mail by phoning 1-888-397-3742. This number will take you to an automated phone system that will guide you through what is required to receive your report. It will tell you the personal information you are required to photocopy and submit. It will also state the fees involved.

Mail all the information to —

Experian
PO Box 2104
Allan, TX 75013

It will take approximately 10 days for your credit report to arrive.

Phone

You cannot get a credit report from Experian by phone. You must call the service number listed in the mail section above and mail in your request along with copies of all required identification and your payment in full, or order online.

Filing a fraud alert with Experian

You can file a fraud alert with Experian either online, by phone, or by mail:

Online

To place a fraud alert online, visit Experian's website at www.experian.com and take the following steps:

1. Click the drop-down menu on the top right of the page and select "United States."

2. Click the link in the menu on your right that says "Steps to take if you are a victim of fraud or identity theft."

On this web page, Experian offers you the option of placing any one of three types of fraud alerts:

Initial Security Alert (90 days)

You can place an "Initial Security Alert" on your file, which lasts for 90 days. When you click on the "Initial Security Alert" link, you'll be taken to an online form that you will have to complete and submit.

Extended Fraud Victim Alert (7 years)

You can place an "Extended Fraud Victim Alert," which will stay on your file for seven years, but you can do this only by mail. When you click on the link that says "Extended Fraud Victim Alert," you will be taken to a form that you must print out, complete, and mail to Experian along with a valid copy of an identity theft report that you've filed with a federal, state, or local law enforcement agency. You also need to include a copy of the first page of your phone bill. It must show your name, address, and home phone number. Finally, you should include a business phone number too.

Active Duty Alert (1 year)

If you are a member of the military on active duty, you can place an "Active Duty Alert" on your file, which will last for 12 months. This type of alert can be renewed as many times as required. When you click the link that says "Active Duty Alert," you will be taken to an online form. Complete it and click "Submit."

Phone

To place a fraud alert with Experian by phone, call 1-888-397-3742 and choose the fraud alert option. This system will allow you to place one of the three types of alerts listed above. This is an automated system that asks for your information by requiring you to enter numbers on the phone keypad. It's very time-consuming, and you must have your identification information, such as your SSN, ready. If you wish to place an Extended Fraud Victim Alert for seven years, this phone system will give you mailing instructions.

Mail

You can place an Initial Security Alert by mail by enclosing the following items:

- A written statement saying you are a victim of fraud that includes your full name, current mailing address, social security number, date of birth, and any previous addresses you've lived at during the last five years. If you do not wish to send all this information by mail, you could request them to contact you by phone upon receipt of your letter. Please remember to state the phone number(s) you would like added to the alert.

- Two proofs of your address, such as copies of a utility bill, insurance statement, driver's license, government benefit statement, military identification, etc.

- A copy of a phone bill in your name clearly displaying one of the two phone numbers that will appear in the victim statement.

Mail this information to —

Experian
PO Box 9556
Allen, TX 75013

CANADIAN CREDIT BUREAUS

There are about 125 credit reporting agencies in Canada. However, the two largest are TransUnion Canada and Equifax Canada. Each of these credit reporting agencies collects and distributes different information, and so you must contact each separately. Since all companies requiring credit information contact these two agencies, they are the only ones you need to place fraud alerts with or request credit reports from.

Fraud alerts

If you are a victim of identity theft, it is important you place a fraud alert with each national credit reporting agency. There is no fee for placing a fraud alert.

The fraud alert will remain on file for five years. If at any time you wish to have the alert removed, you can submit a written request.

Forms and sample letters to assist you in dealing with the credit reporting agencies are available in Chapter 6 and also on the enclosed CD.

TransUnion Canada

TransUnion is one of the two major credit reporting agencies in Canada. Remember, though, that you must order reports from both agencies to get the full picture of your credit situation.

Credit file request

If you suspect that you are a victim of identity theft, or want to confirm that you are not a victim, request a copy of your credit file from TransUnion Canada.

Online

An immediate copy of your credit report can be requested from TransUnion Canada's website for a fee of $14.99, including taxes.

To get a copy of your credit report online, take these steps:

1. Log on to www.transunion.ca and choose your language.

2. Click "Personal Solutions" from their menu at the top of the page.

3. Click "Order Credit Report & Score" from the menu on the left side of the page.

4. Click "Option One."

5. Click "Order Now."

6. Complete all the forms and submit.

You will need to give TransUnion the following personal information:

- Social insurance number

- Date of birth

- Current address

- Previous address (if you have moved within the past two years)

- One of your credit card numbers (for example, Master-Card, Visa, American Express) and your credit limit

- Installment loan account number, if you have an installment loan (for example, student, auto, jewelry, or furniture loan)

Mail

If you wish to request a report by mail, you can complete Trans-Union Canada's information form on the following page and mail it to the appropriate address below. (The form is also available at www.tuscores.ca/Personal/consumerRelationsForm.jsp ?locale=en_CA.) Your credit report will be mailed to you via Canada Post. If you order your report by mail, there is no cost.

For Canadian residents outside Quebec:

TransUnion
Consumer Relations Centre
PO Box 338, LCD 1
Hamilton, ON L8L 7W2

For Quebec residents:

TransUnion (Echo Group)
Suite 370
1 Place Laval
Laval, QC H7N 1A1

SAMPLE CREDIT FILE REQUEST FORM FROM TRANSUNION

CONSUMER RELATIONS - INFORMATION FORM

To enable our associates to ID your file and yourself, please print, then complete this form in full and mail it to the address provided on www.tuc.ca. Your request must also include both sides of two pieces of photocopied identification, one must include a signature (see instructions on our website).

Please Print

Personal Information

Last Name:	First Name:	
Middle Name:	Date of Birth:	JR/SR
SIN (optional)	Home Phone (optional)	

Address Information

Present Address		Apt. #
City	Province	Postal Code	How Long?

Previous Address (if present is less than 2 years)		Apt. #
City	Province	Postal Code	How Long?

Employment History (optional)

Present or Previous Employer	How Long?

I am the person named above and I understand that I could be prosecuted under federal or provincial legislation for obtaining information from a consumer reporting agency by fraudulent means or under false pretences.

Signature	Date

REPRINTED WITH PERMISSION.

TransUnion requires a photocopy of both sides of two pieces of identification from the list below. The pieces of identification you choose to photocopy must include your name, current address, date of birth, and signature.

Acceptable identification includes any two of the following:

- Driver's license
- Canadian passport
- Certificate of Indian status

- Citizenship and immigration form

- Department of National Defence card

- Signed credit card (primary account holder)

- Permanent residence card

- Old Age Security card

Alternatively, you may include one of the above, along with one of the following:

- Birth certificate

- Social insurance card

- T4 slip

- CNB card

- Utility bill showing your current address (must be no more than 60 days old)

- Credit card bill showing your current address (must be no more than 60 days old)

Phone

TransUnion Canada does not allow you to order a credit report by phone. You must order online or by mail.

If more than one member of your household is requesting a file, each individual must supply a separate request and include all the above information.

Ordering in person

You can also drop into a local TransUnion Canada office if there is one in your city. They have offices in Toronto, Vancouver, Edmonton, Calgary, Saskatoon, Montreal, Quebec City, Rimouski, Moncton, Charlottetown, Dartmouth, and St. John's. Each location is listed in the White Pages. They ask that you phone them first to book an appointment. They will also ask you to bring two pieces of identification that contain your current name and address.

The following pages contain a sample of a credit report from the TransUnion website.

SAMPLE CREDIT REPORT FROM TRANSUNION (CANADA)

① Your Name and Current Address

DOE, JOHN J.
123 NOWHERE ST.
WONDERLAND, ON M1B5N1

Date of Report: 09/30/2002
② Case Number: 104452642

Use this unique identifier to refer to this credit report if you contact customer support.

Personal Data:

③ Previous Address(es)

Former Addresses Reported:
321 NOPLACE RD.
GREATWORLD, ON M9R1L9

Social Insurance Number: on file
Reported Date of Birth: 08/01/1970
You have been in our files since: 10/1988
AKA: DOE, JOHN
Phone Number: (123) 456-7890

④ Your Personal Information

Employment Data:

Employer: NONAME INC.
Position: MANAGER

Province: ON
Date Reported: 09/2002

Satisfactory Account Information Section

⑤ List of account(s) with no Adverse Information

The following accounts are reported with no adverse information.

⑥ Provider of Account Information

ABCD BANK   Revolving account

Revised Date: 09/2002   **Balance:** $678.00   Joint

⑧ The date this account opened

Opened: 03/1996   **Payment Terms:** Monthly $0.00

⑦ Account types can include installment loans, credit cards, auto loans, retail accounts, and finance company accounts.

Last Day of Activity: 02/2002   **Past Due:** $0.00   **Credit Limit:** $5,000.00

Remarks: Remarks go here.

Status as of 09/2002
In prior 36 month(s) from date of last activity, never late

Adverse Account Information Section

⑨ Credit report information that is not considered to be positive payment behavior, such as a past due account, remark code, or late payment history. See 8.

The following accounts contain information, which some creditors may consider to be adverse. Adverse account information may generally be reported for 7 years from the date of the first delinquency, depending on your province of residence. The adverse information in these accounts has been printed in >brackets< for your convenience, to help you understand your report. They are not bracketed this way for creditors.

XYZ INC.   Installment account

Revised date: 09/2002   **Balance:** $200.00   Individual

Opened: 05/1989   **Payment Terms:** Monthly $80.00

Last Day of Activity: 12/1997   **Past Due:** $0.00   **Credit Limit:** $1,000.00

Remarks: Remarks go here.

Status as of 12/1997
In prior 36 month(s) from date of last activity, never late

10 Information obtained from public records.

Derogatory Public Record

The following items obtained from public records appear on your report. You may be required to explain these items to potential creditors. For example, bankruptcy information reports for 6 to 7 years from discharge date or 14 years from filing date, depending on the province. Legal items may report on your file for 6 to 10 years, depending on the province. We encourage you to check your provincial legislation for full details on the reporting periods for negative information.

Bankruptcy Information

Date Revised:	08/2002
Reference Number:	32132132
Division Information:	456456
Court Filing Number:	45456
Date Reported:	05/2000
Date Discharged:	01/2002
Assets:	$3,000.00
Liabilities:	$35,000.00
Bankruptcy Discharge Type:	Automatic Discharge
Bankruptcy Status:	Comment about the bankruptcy status is shown here.
Trustee's Name:	Sample Trustee
Trustee's Company Name:	Sample Trustee Company, Inc.
Additional Information:	Additional information is shown here.
Remark:	Comment about the bankruptcy is shown here.

Legal Items

Date Revised:	09/2002
Plaintiff:	Plaintiff Name
Legal Type:	Judgement
Case Number:	45546456
Court Type:	Small Claims Court
Court Location:	Greatworld, ON
Date Reported:	09/2002
Date Satisfied:	11/2002
Original Amount:	$5,000.00
Current Balance:	$0.00
Status:	Comment about the status is shown here.
Lawyer:	Sample Lawyer Name
Third Party:	Sample Third Party Name
Remark 1:	Comment about the legal item is shown here.
Remark 2:	Comment about the legal item is shown here.

SAMPLE CREDIT REPORT FROM TRANSUNION (CANADA) — CONTINUED

(11) Information obtained from public records.

Non-Derogatory Public Record

The following items obtained from public records appear on your report. You may be required to explain these items to potential creditors. The items listed are any liens or collateral assignments registered in your name.

Subscriber Name:	HSBC Bank Canada
Date Filed:	12/2000
Maturity Date:	04/2005
Original Balance:	$50,000.00
Security:	Consumer Goods
Registration Number:	4564456456
Remark 1:	Comment about the legal item is shown here.
Remark 2:	Comment about the legal item is shown here.

(12) Collection information reported to TransUnion.

Collections Section

The following items listed are any collections that have been reported on your file. Adverse account information may generally be reported for 6 or 7 years from the date reported, depending on your province of residence.

Collections Information

Collection Agency Name:	XYZ COLLECTIONS
Account Number:	123abc456def789
Creditor's Name:	FACTORY SHOES
Date Reported:	06/2002
Date Revised:	08/2002
Status Date:	11/2002
Original Balance:	$1,500.00
Current Balance:	$0.00
Remarks:	Some comments about the collection are shown here.

SAMPLE CREDIT REPORT FROM TRANSUNION (CANADA) — CONTINUED

13 Non-sufficient funds information reported to TransUnion.

Non-Sufficient Fund Information

This section lists any non-sufficient funds cheques that have been reported.

Company Name:	CDF Company
Dishonoured Date:	10/2002
Date Reported:	10/2002
Remark:	N.S.F./NON SUFFICIENT FUNDS
Balance:	$100.00
Status:	N.S.F./NON SUFFICIENT FUNDS
Verification Number:	1A2B3C

14 Non-sufficient fund information reported to TransUnion.

Consumer Statement Section

No Consumer Statements on file

15 Companies who are deciding if they should offer you credit may make regular inquiries. These inquiries affect your credit report and score.

Regular Inquiry Section

The following companies have received your credit report. (Note) Transunion consumer disclosure inquiries are not viewed by creditors.)

Date	Subscriber Name
09/25/2002	ZYX FINANCIAL CORP
09/20/2002	TU CONSUMER DISCLOSURE
08/25/2002	CREDIT DATA/SOMEONE CORP.

16 Companies who have an existing relationship with you may make account review inquiries. These inquiries do not affect your credit report and score.

Account Management Inquiry Section

Credit grantors who have permission to review credit histories and payment habits of their account holders may do so on a periodic basis. Account management inquiries are disclosed only to the consumer and not to other credit grantors.

Date	Subscriber Name
09/18/2002	TRANS UNION SCORE
08/04/2002	ABCD BANK

End of Report Section

If you believe any of the information in your credit report is incorrect, please let us know. Please address all correspondence regarding your credit report to:

TransUnion Canada

Consumer Relations

P.O. Box 338, LCD 1

Hamilton, ON

L8L 7W2

Filing a fraud alert with TransUnion Canada

If, when you check your report, you notice anything suspicious, immediately file a fraud alert. All fraud alerts are free.

To contact the fraud department for TransUnion Canada, all residents of Canada except those living in Quebec should phone 1-877-525-3823 between 8:00 a.m. and 8:00 p.m. EST. You should be aware that you may have to wait for up to 30 minutes to talk to someone.

Because all of Quebec's records are kept separate, if you live in Quebec, you must phone 1-877-713-3393 or (514) 335-0374.

TransUnion requests that you have your SIN or credit card number handy before you make the call. They will take all the necessary information and will send you a fraud package to assist you.

The fraud alert will stay on your file for five years. Should you apply for credit, the creditor will call you to verify that it is really you making the application. Therefore, ensure your contact information at TransUnion is always accurate.

When I asked TransUnion's fraud department for advice about identity theft, they stated, "Please tell the public not to carry their social insurance cards and birth certificates in their wallets." They strongly recommend that you keep these cards locked in a safe place unless you need them. They have seen the problems the theft of SIN cards and birth certificates can cause.

Equifax Canada

Equifax Canada is the other national credit reporting agency in Canada. It is important you contact Equifax in addition to Trans-Union Canada. No credit reporting agency will contact another one on your behalf.

Credit file request

You can request your credit file from Equifax by any one of the following three methods:

Online

You can request an online copy of your credit report for a fee of $14.99 including taxes.

To get a copy of your credit report from Equifax online, follow these steps:

1. Log on to www.equifax.ca.

2. Click "Consumer Information Centre" in the left menu.

3. Click "Your Credit Report" in the left menu.

4. Click "Purchase Your Credit Report On-line for $14.50" at the bottom of the page.

5. Click "Order Now" at the bottom of the page.

6. Click "Register a New Account."

7. Complete the forms and click "Submit."

Phone

You can phone for a report at 1-800-465-7166. Once you have placed your request, they will mail your report to you.

Mail

You can receive a free copy of your credit report by mailing your request to Equifax.

Be sure to include —

- your full name,

- current and former addresses for the last two years,

- date of birth,

- SIN (not mandatory),

- photocopies of two pieces of identification, such as a driver's license or birth certificate, and

- proof of your current address such as copies of your telephone bill or utility bills that show your address and phone number.

Send the information to —

National Consumer Relations
PO Box 190
Jean-Talon Station
Montreal, QC H1S 2Z2

Your report will be mailed to you.

Filing a fraud alert with Equifax Canada

To place a fraud alert with Equifax Canada, call them at 1-800-465-7166. This number operates 24 hours a day, seven days a week. It takes you to an automated system that will prompt you for information and will immediately put a flag on your account indicating that you may be the victim of identity theft. You will need to have your SIN and a credit card number available. The automated system will also ask for address information.

Once all the data is taken, a representative will call you back.

They will add a statement to your file to alert credit grantors that you may be a victim of fraud.

Equifax does warn you that this may mean that the next time you apply for credit, you may be questioned more thoroughly. The credit grantor wants to make sure that you are, in fact, the person you say you are.

It's Safer to Order a Credit Report by Phone than Online

There are a number of websites that offer free annual credit reports. However, the World Privacy Forum (WPF), a nonprofit organization that investigates and reports on privacy and technology issues, recently released a report stating that there was a 100 percent increase in fake credit-report sites. These sites, which show up in web-search results, try to trick users into releasing their personal information by getting them to fill in a form on the site. Unfortunately, the sole purpose of these sites is to steal personal information.

It's still best to order your credit report by telephone. However, if you do choose to order a free annual report through a website, protect yourself by taking the following steps:

- Ensure you are running an Internet security program like Norton Internet Security. This will prevent fake websites from placing illegal programs, like viruses, on your computer.

- Don't use a computer in a public place like an Internet café or a library. These computers may not be protected, and your information could be intercepted or stolen.

- Don't use a computer at work. Some employers monitor and record all Internet activity.

- If you do choose to go online to access your free credit report, be very careful when you type in the website address. A single character mistake could place you at a fake website.

- If you call for your report, or have it mailed to you, ensure that your credit report is mailed to a secure mailbox.

6

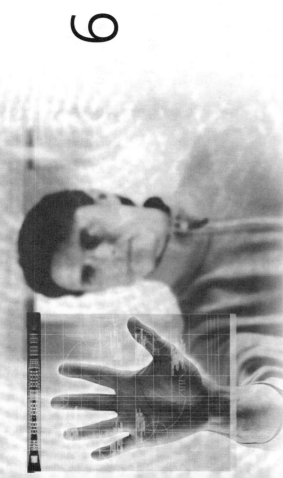

FORMS FOR DEALING WITH IDENTITY THEFT

The forms on the following pages will assist you when you contact the police, your creditors, government departments, and the credit reporting agencies to inform them that your identity has been stolen.

Use these forms to record the details of whom you talk to and what the results of that conversation were. If you aren't happy with the response you're getting from the person you're dealing with, go higher up in the organization. Ask to speak with a supervisor or manager. Keep trying until you reach someone who can assist you.

As problems resulting from the theft of your identity can occur years after you've discovered the theft, be sure to keep copies of all correspondence you send out in your efforts to repair the situation.

The following forms are included on the CD-ROM in both MS Word and PDF formats.

ID Theft Victim Information Form

Use this form to document your situation. Copies can be given to credit reporting agencies and law enforcement if necessary.

Contact Checklist

Use this form to list all the organizations you need to contact. As you contact each one, check it off.

Law Enforcement Contact Form

Use this form to record your contact with law enforcement agencies.

Financial Institutions Contact Forms

Use these forms to contact all your financial organizations:

- Main Financial Institutions Contact Form
- Additional Financial Contacts Form
- Credit Card Companies Contact Form
- Department Stores Contact Form

Government Organizations

Use these forms to contact government departments:

- Driver's License Contact Form
- SSN or SIN Information Contact Form
- Passport Contact Form

Utilities

Use these forms to contact utility companies and service providers:

- Telephone Companies Contact Form
- Utility Companies Contact Form
- Other Services Contact Form

Miscellaneous Forms

- Post Office Contact Form
- Medical Information Contact Form

Credit Reporting Agencies

Use these forms to contact the appropriate credit reporting agencies for your country:

- Equifax United States
- TransUnion United States
- Experian United States
- Equifax Canada
- TransUnion Canada

Sample Letters

These sample letters are on the enclosed CD in Word files so that you can edit them in a word processor.

- Sample Letter to a Credit Reporting Agency
- Sample Letter to Existing Creditors
- Sample Confirmation Letter

Quick Lists of Contacts

These forms are for quick reference of your most important contacts.

- Quick List of US Contacts
- Quick List of Canadian Contacts

ID Theft Victim Information Form

Victim Information

Name at time of incident

First name _____

Middle name or initial _____

Last name _____

Name (if changed since incident)

First name _____

Middle name or initial _____

Last name _____

Birth date _____

Address at time of incident

Street _____

City _____

State/province _____

ZIP/postal code _____

Current address (if different from above)

Street _____

City _____

State/province _____

ZIP/postal code _____

Current contact information

Home phone _____

Cell phone _____

Work phone _____

Other phone _____

Fax _____

E-mail _____

Particulars of Incident

This incident happened on or about *(Enter the date)*	
An identity thief used my personal information without my permission.	Yes [ ] No [ ]
I received no benefits of any kind from this incident.	Yes [ ] No [ ]
My personal information was	Stolen [ ] Lost [ ]
I do *not* know who stole my personal information.	True [ ] False [ ]

I suspect the following person is responsible for stealing and using my personal information: *(Complete all known information.)*

First name _____

Middle name or initial _____

Last name _____

The suspect is a relative   Yes [ ]   No [ ]

Relationship _____

Address *(if known)*

Street _____

City _____

State/province _____

ZIP/postal code _____

Phone number(s) *(if known)*

Home phone _____

Cell phone _____

Work phone _____

Other phone _____

Fax _____

Additional information about the suspect: *(for example, how you think the suspect committed the crime, is the suspect a friend, how you know the suspect, why you believe he or she is responsible, etc.)*

Legal Considerations

I have given a copy of this form to a law enforcement agency.	Yes [ ] No [ ]
The police wrote a report and gave me a copy of it.	Yes [ ] No [ ]
I will act as a witness if necessary.	Yes [ ] No [ ]
This form can be used in any way to prosecute the person who stole my personal information.	Yes [ ] No [ ]

Particulars of Police Report

Name of law enforcement agency (i.e., RCMP, state, or local police)	
Name of person taking the report	
Date the report was taken	
Phone number for law enforcement office	
Report file number	
I received a copy of the report.	Yes [ ] No [ ]

Details of incident: *(State how the thief used your information and give any particulars that might assist law enforcement officials in furthering your case.)*

Documents

I have attached copies of the following documents:

State- or province-issued ID card	[ ]
Passport	[ ]
Driver's license	[ ]
Birth certificate	[ ]
A copy of the police report	[ ]
The police report file number (if the report is not attached)	[ ]
Other:	

Signature

I swear that to the best of my knowledge the information I have provided on this form is true.

_____
(Signature)

_____
(Date: Month/Day/Year)

_____
(Notary)

Witness

Note: Your creditors, as well as some other organizations, may want you to have this form notarized. If that is not the case, have one witness of legal age sign below to verify that he or she saw you sign this form. Your witness cannot be a relative.

_____   _____
(Signature)   *(Print name)*

_____   _____
(Date)   *(Telephone number)*

Contact Checklist

Create a list of every organization you have to contact. Use it to record the contacts you have made and to remind you of which ones you still have to notify. Use the "Other Contacts" sheet at the end of this form to list all other companies or agencies you need to contact.

Contact	Contact completed	Contact not required
Federal Trade Commission (US)	[ ]	[ ]
PhoneBusters Canada	[ ]	[ ]
Police department (including criminal records search)	[ ]	[ ]
Financial institutions	[ ]	[ ]
Credit card companies	[ ]	[ ]
Credit reporting agencies	[ ]	[ ]
Check-verification companies	[ ]	[ ]
Department store credit card services	[ ]	[ ]
Department of Motor Vehicles	[ ]	[ ]
Post office	[ ]	[ ]
Investment agencies	[ ]	[ ]
Passport office	[ ]	[ ]
Telephone companies	[ ]	[ ]
Utility companies	[ ]	[ ]
Social Security (US) or HRSDC office (Canada) (issuers of SSN/SIN cards)	[ ]	[ ]
Tax department	[ ]	[ ]
Internet service provider	[ ]	[ ]
Student loan provider	[ ]	[ ]
US trustee or Office of the Superintendent of Bankruptcy Canada	[ ]	[ ]
Old Age Security (OAS) office	[ ]	[ ]

List any other contacts you must make here:

Other contacts	Contact completed	Contact not required
	[ ]	[ ]
	[ ]	[ ]
	[ ]	[ ]
	[ ]	[ ]
	[ ]	[ ]
	[ ]	[ ]
	[ ]	[ ]
	[ ]	[ ]
	[ ]	[ ]
	[ ]	[ ]
	[ ]	[ ]
	[ ]	[ ]
	[ ]	[ ]
	[ ]	[ ]
	[ ]	[ ]
	[ ]	[ ]
	[ ]	[ ]
	[ ]	[ ]
	[ ]	[ ]

Law Enforcement Contact Form

Use this form to record the results of contacting the local law enforcement agency.

Local police department name and address	
Phone number	
Date contacted	
Contact person	
Report or file number	
Comments	
Is a personal visit to the police department necessary?	[ ]
Documents sent or given to the officer	
Follow-up date	

Main Financial Institutions Contact Form

Use this form to record the results of your contacts with banks and credit unions.

Your account number			
Name of financial institution			
Phone number			
Address			
Date contacted			
Person contacted			
Comments			
Documents sent			
Is a personal visit to the bank/credit union necessary?	[ ]	[ ]	[ ]
Notarization required (Yes or no)			
Follow-up date			

Additional Financial Contacts Form

Use this form to record the results of any contacts you make with other financial institutions or companies, such as student loan providers or check-cashing companies.

Company name			
Phone number			
Address			
Date contacted			
Person contacted			
Comments			
Is a personal visit to the financial institution/company necessary?	[ ]	[ ]	[ ]
Documents sent			[ ]
Notarization required (Yes or no)			
Follow-up date			

Credit Card Companies Contact Form

Use this form to record your contacts with credit card companies.

Your credit card number			
Name of credit card company			
Phone number			
Address			
Date contacted			
Person contacted			
Comments			
Documents sent			
Notarization required (Yes or no)			
Follow-up date			

Department Stores Contact Form

Use this form to record your contacts with department store accounts.

Your account number	Name of department store	Phone number	Address	Date contacted	Person contacted	Comments	Documents sent	Notarization required (Yes or no)	Follow-up date

Driver's License Contact Form

Use this form if you think someone is using a driver's license in your name.

Your driver's license number	
Department name	
Phone number	
Address	
Person contacted	
Date contacted	
Comments	
Is a personal visit to the department necessary?	[ ]
Documents sent or given to the department (if necessary)	
Notarization required (Yes or no)	
Follow-up date	

SSN or SIN Information Contact Form

Use this form to discover or correct information if you suspect someone has a SSN or SIN card in your name.

Your social security or social insurance number	
Department name	
Phone number	
Address	
Date contacted	
Person contacted	
Comments	
Is a personal visit to the Social Security office or HRSDC office necessary?	[ ]
Documents sent or given to the office (if necessary)	
Notarization required (Yes or no)	
Follow-up date	

Passport Contact Form

Use this form if you think someone has a passport in your name.

Your passport number	
Department name	
Phone number	
Address	
Person contacted	
Date contacted	
Comments	
Is a personal visit to the office necessary?	[ ]
Documents sent or given to the office (if necessary)	
Notarization required (Yes or no)	
Follow-up date	

Telephone Companies Contact Form

Use this form to record your contacts with telephone companies.

	Home phone	Cell phone	Fax number
Your account number			
Company name			
Phone number			
Address			
Date contacted			
Person contacted			
Comments			
Documents sent			
Notarization required (Yes or no)			
Follow-up date			

Utility Companies Contact Form

Use this form to record your contacts with utility providers.

	Electricity	Heat	Water
Your account number			
Company name			
Phone number			
Address			
Date contacted			
Person contacted			
Comments			
Documents sent			
Notarization required (Yes or no)			
Follow-up date			

Other Services Contact Form

Use this form to contact any companies providing you with services such as cable or satellite television.

Your account number			
Company name			
Phone number			
Address			
Date contacted			
Person contacted			
Comments			
Documents sent			
Notarization required (Yes or no)			
Follow-up date			

Post Office Contact Form

Use this form to record your contacts with the post office to ensure that no one has changed your mailing address.

Phone number	
Address	
Date contacted	
Person contacted	
Comments	
Is a personal visit to the post office necessary?	[ ]
Documents sent or given to the post office (if necessary)	
Notarization required (Yes or no)	
Follow-up date	

Medical Information Contact Form

Use this form to contact any medical organizations you may deal with, such as a health insurance plan in the United States or a provincial medical services plan in Canada.

Your medical card number	
Department name	
Phone number	
Address	
Date contacted	
Person contacted	
Comments	
Is a personal visit to the office necessary?	[ ]
Documents sent or given to the department (if necessary)	
Notarization required (Yes or no)	
Follow-up date	

Equifax United States Contact Form

Use this form to record the steps you've taken to report the fraudulent use of your identity to Equifax. Keep this form in a safe place for reference.

Phone number: 1-888-766-0008	
Date contacted	
Contact person	
Comments	
Documents sent	
Follow-up date	

TransUnion United States Contact Form

Use this form to record the steps you've taken to report the fraudulent use of your identity to TransUnion. Keep this form in a safe place for reference.

Phone number: 1-800-680-7289	
Date contacted	
Contact person	
Comments	
Documents sent	
Follow-up date	

Experian United States Contact Form

Use this form to record the steps you've taken to report the fraudulent use of your identity to Experian. Keep this form in a safe place for reference.

Phone number: 1-888-397-3742	
Date contacted	
Contact person	
Comments	
Documents sent	
Follow-up date	

Equifax Canada Contact Form

Use this form to record the steps you've taken to report the fraudulent use of your identity to Equifax. Keep this form in a safe place for reference.

Phone number: 1-800-465-7166	
Date contacted	
Contact person	
Comments	
Documents sent	
Follow-up date	

TransUnion Canada Contact Form

Use this form to record the steps you've taken to report the fraudulent use of your identity to TransUnion. Keep this form in a safe place for reference.

Phone number: 1-877-525-3823 (Quebec: 1-877-713-3393)	
Date contacted	
Contact person	
Comments	
Documents sent	
Follow-up date	

Sample Letter to a Credit Reporting Agency

Date

Complaint department
Name of credit reporting agency
Street address
City, state/province, ZIP/postal code

Dear Sir or Madam:

I am writing to inform you that I am a victim of identity theft.

I have enclosed a copy of my credit report dated *(insert date of report)* and circled the entries that I am disputing. I have no knowledge of these entries and would like them removed from my file.

Should you need to contact me for further clarification or to answer any questions, you can reach me at the following e-mail address and phone numbers:

(Insert your e-mail address.)
(Insert your phone numbers.)

I have enclosed the following documents to verify my claim:

(List any documents you have enclosed.)

Sincerely,

Your name
Your street address
Your city, state/province, ZIP/postal code

Sample Letter to Existing Creditors

Date

Complaint department
Name of creditor
Street address
City, state/province, ZIP/postal code

Dear Sir or Madam:

I am writing to inform you that I am a victim of identity theft.

I have enclosed a copy of my statement and circled the entries that I am disputing. I have no knowledge of these transactions and would like them removed from my file.

Should you need to contact me for further clarification or to answer any questions, you can reach me at the following e-mail address and phone numbers:

(Insert your e-mail address.)
(Insert your phone numbers.)

I have enclosed the following documents to verify my claim:

(List any documents you have enclosed.)

Sincerely,

Your name
Your street address
Your city, state/province, ZIP/postal code

Sample Confirmation Letter

Date

Complaint department
Name of company
Street address
City, state/province, ZIP/postal code

Dear Sir or Madam:

I am writing to confirm our phone call of *(insert date and time of conversation)*. As we discussed, I am a victim of identity theft and am attempting to correct my personal information with your company. If you have requested any documents, I have enclosed them with this letter as requested.

Please contact me immediately should you have any further questions or require more information. I can be reached at the above address, or you can phone me during business hours at *(insert your phone number)*.

If I do not hear from you within 30 days of sending this letter, I will contact you to confirm that this matter is settled.

Thank you for your assistance.

Sincerely,

Your name
Your street address
Your city, state/province, ZIP/postal code

Enclosures: *(List all documents you are enclosing.)*

Quick List of US Contacts

This list is to give you fast access to the contact information in this book.

Credit Reporting Agencies

Company	Credit Report Request	Consumer Fraud Division	Website
Equifax	1-800-685-1111	1-888-766-0008	www.equifax.com
TransUnion	1-800-888-4213	1-800-680-7289	www.transunion.com
Experian	Not available by phone.	1-888-397-3742	www.experian.com

Check-cashing Companies

Company	Credit Report Request	Website
TeleCheck	1-800-710-9898	www.telecheck.com
Global Payments Check Service	1-866-860-9061	www.globalpaymentsinc.com
Certegy Inc.	1-800-437-5120	www.certegy.com

Other Contacts

Organization	Phone number	Website
Federal Trade Commission	1-877-ID-THEFT	www.consumer.gov/idtheft
Securities and Exchange Commission	(202) 942-7040	www.sec.gov/complaint.shtml
IRS	1-800-829-0433	www.irs.gov/file/index.html
Social Security Administration	1-800-772-1213	www.ssa.gov
US Department of State	1-877-487-2778	www.travel.state.gov/passport/passport_1738.html
Federal Communications Commission	1-888-CALL-FCC	www.fcc.gov

Quick List of Canadian Contacts

This list is to give you fast access to the contact information in this book.

Credit Reporting Agencies

Company	Credit Report Request	Consumer Fraud Division	Website
Equifax	1-800-465-7166	1-800-465-7166	www.equifax.ca
TransUnion (English Canada)	Not available by phone.	1-877-525-3823	www.transunion.ca
TransUnion (Quebec)	Not available by phone.	1-877-713-3393	www.transunion.ca

Other Contacts

Organization	Phone number	Website
Telecheck	1-800-366-2425	www.telecheck.com
Certegy Inc.	1-800-770-3792	www.certegy.com
Investment Dealers Association of Canada	1-877-442-4322	www.ida.ca
PhoneBusters	1-888-495-8501	www.phonebusters.com
Canada Revenue Agency	Call your local office listed in the blue pages of your phone book.	www.cra-arc.gc.ca
Canada Revenue Agency Investigations Unit	Call your local office listed in the blue pages of your phone book.	www.cra-arc.gc.ca/agency/investigations/province_tax-e.html
Canada Pension Plan and Old Age Security	For service in English: 1-800-277-9914 For service in French: 1-800-277-9915	www.sdc.gc.ca/en/isp/common/proceed/vupipns.shtml
Canada Firearms Centre	1-800-731-4000	www.cfc-ccaf.gc.ca
Canadian Radio-Television and Telecommunications Commission (CRTC)	1-877-249-2782	www.crtc.gc.ca

ALSO OF INTEREST FROM SELF-COUNSEL PRESS

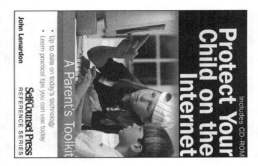

Protect Your Child on the Internet
A Parent's Toolkit

John Lenardon
ISBN 10: 1-55180-688-6
ISBN 13: 978-1-55180-688-4
$12.95 US / $15.95 CDN

The Internet has become an important part of most children's lives, allowing them to learn and explore a wealth of knowledge about every topic in the world. For many children, it has also become the main communication line to their friends. But this technology is inherent with dangers. *Protect Your Child on the Internet* explains what those dangers are and how you can protect your children.

This book describes, in non-technical language, how you can see where your children have been surfing on the Net, and how to block what can hurt them. It shows parents what the dangers are and provides simple solutions so that parents can make the Internet a fun and exciting experience for their children. Topics include:

- Dangers of the World Wide Web
- Chat room concerns and solutions
- Webcam concerns and solutions
- How cyber bullies bully
- E-mail "phishing" dangers
- Newsgroup dangers

Protect Your Child on the Internet includes forms and checklists and teaches you practical tips you can use today.